Checkered Flag Teams

Driving Your Workplace Into the Winner's Circle

RENÉE MERCHANT
and JO ELLEN ROE

Illustrated by Robert Hudgins

FIRST EDITION

Gold and Silver Press
Ann Arbor, Michigan

Checkered Flag Teams:
Driving Your Workplace Into the Winner's Circle

Written by Renée Merchant and Jo Ellen Roe
Illustrated by Robert Hudgins

Unattributed quotations are by either Renée Merchant or Jo Ellen Roe.

Printed in the United States of America

Publisher's Cataloging-in-Publication Data
(Provided by Quality Books, Inc.)

Merchant, Renee.
Checkered flag teams : driving your workplace
to the winner's circle / written by Renee Merchant
and Jo Ellen Roe ; illustrated by Robert Hudgins
— 1st ed.
p. cm.
Includes bibliographical references and index.
LCCN: 00-104797
ISBN: 0-9701390-2-0

1. Teams in the workplace—Management.
2. Indusrial project management. I. Roe, Jo
Ellen. II. Title.

HD66.M47 2000   658.4'036
                                 QBI00-500150

Library of Congress Number: 00-104797

ISBN 0-9701390-2-0

Published by:
Gold and Silver Press
4313 Joy Road West
Ann Arbor, MI 48105 U.S.A
orders@goldandsilverpress.com
http://www.goldandsilverpress.com
http://www.4DeltaSystems.com

To Dick Merchant and Chuck Roe,
our teammates of long standing

CONTENTS

ACKNOWLEDGEMENTS

The authors wish to thank the following people:

- All those who gave generously of their time and talent to review this manuscript and offer wonderful suggestions to make it better: Rosalie Bargmann, Tommy Cameron, Kathie Dannemiller, Greg Huszczo, Ned Jarrett, Cindy Krieg, Melanie Love, Susan Mills, Shelly Pfister, Dale Schreiner, Bill Smith, and Linda Stiles.

- All those who granted us personal interviews: Kevin Androsian, Dean Daugharthy, Ned Jarrett, George Winchester, and Russ Yeager.

- Dr. James Conley, Professor Emeritus at the College of Business at Eastern Michigan University, for suggesting it was time to write a book; and Michael Scott Karpovich, Certified Speaking Professional, for inspiring Renée to "leave a legacy."

- Dr. Greg Huszczo and Dr. Mary Vielhaber, professors in the College of Business at Eastern Michigan University who taught us about organizational development. We appreciate their concern for us as students and for the organizations with which we work.

- All those who contributed to the final look of the book: Doug Bentley for careful and precise editing;

Robert Hudgins for wonderful pen and ink drawings, and Sans Serif for design.

- Finally, our families: particularly Dick Merchant, for his insight, creative ideas, patience, and careful computer work; Chuck Roe, for listening and offering surprising nuggets of wisdom in his characteristically understated way; and Nan, Bob, Nick, Melanie, Michael, and Holly, for being a great family team.

DISCLAIMER

This book provides information on ways to build teams and help them achieve checkered flag results. It is sold with the understanding that the publisher and authors are not rendering legal, counseling or consulting services. If the reader needs legal or other expert help, including the services of a counselor or a consultant, he or she should seek a competent professional.

This book makes no claim to be an exhaustive resource for building teams or to substitute for other books about teams. Instead, its purpose is to complement, amplify and supplement other texts.

The art of building teams is not an exact science, and no team-building method can guarantee specific results. Building a good team and achieving the results the team sets out to achieve requires a significant investment of time and energy by all involved. No magic bullet exists that will instantly produce results—and this book makes no claims to be such a magic bullet.

All quotations from race drivers and others associated with racing, other team sports or experts in building teams were taken from previously published sources, with the exception of the personal interviews.

The authors and the publisher have made every effort to make this book as complete and accurate as possible. However, there may be mistakes, both typographical and in content. Please use the text as a guide but not as an infallible resource. The book contains information on team building that is current only up to the printing date.

INTRODUCTION

Checkered Flag Teams is based primarily on the work of Renée Merchant, owner for 18 years of Delta Systems, a team-building company that works with people who want a faster way to build their team and with team leaders who want to energize existing teams. Satisfied clients include Ford Motor Company, Visteon, TENNECO Automotive, Aeroquip Corporation, Armour Swift-Eckrich, Detroit Edison, Fermi 2 Nuclear Power Plant, the State of Michigan, the University of Michigan, and the Texas Workforce Commission.

Using the metaphor of auto racing, this how-to manual pulls wit and wisdom from the National Association for Stock Car Auto Racing (NASCAR®) and other racing groups to illustrate teamwork principles. It is a resource for managers, team leaders, team members, consultants, trainers and entrepreneurs who want a fast, effective way to build successful, productive teams. It contains chapters that guide a team in seeing the "winner's circle," running the "teamwork race," and finally, reflecting on their run for the purpose of continuous improvement. It describes the stages all teams go through and offers more than 30 Fast Start Teamwork™ tools that have helped numerous teams in a variety of settings develop synergy and take the checkered flag.

In auto racing, to "take the checkered flag" means to complete the race. All racing teams want to be the first to cross the finish line and earn a trip to the winner's circle to celebrate. In contrast, business teams within an organization are ideally not competing *against* each other. These teams take the checkered flag when they achieve their vision together. Successful business teams do not "win" every time. Rather, they complete the process, gain knowledge and expertise in working effectively together, and learn how to do it better next time.

While the book focuses on teams at work that achieve outstanding results, the information, tools and activities it contains can help build strong home teams and effective community teams as well. The final chapter describes a few of these successful teams.

We hope you find *Checkered Flag Teams* interesting to read and fun to use. And we hope that because you've read and learned from it, you and your teammates will consistently take the checkered flag.

Racing Toward Teamwork

1

Thinking About Teams

"I think teamwork is the most important thing you learn in any sort of sport. Certainly in racing you need a driver. You need a crew chief. You need a number of people. You need everyone. No one sits at the top of the pile."

—Roger Penske, former race driver and team owner

Teamwork Is a Common Business Strategy

In the business world these days, teams are everywhere. Businesses commonly use teams to drive productivity and results. *Fortune* lists teamwork as "a key priority" of the world's most admired companies. "Its defining unit is teamwork," says *Fast Company*, describing a fast and agile modern organization. Teamwork is as important on the racetrack as it is in the business world. No race event at the Michigan International Speedway or any other racetrack could possibly succeed without teams. As Ned Jarrett, two-time Winston Cup champion, says, "I can't think of anything major that anyone has accomplished by themselves. There is always someone else involved, and that is teamwork. We see it everyday on a race team. The drivers get most of the credit, but they know in their hearts that they're just one spoke in the wheel."

RACING WISDOM

"Racing is a team sport. Everyone who races pretty much has the same car and the same equipment. What sets us apart is our people. I like to talk about our 'team IQ'—because none of us is as smart as all of us."

—Ray Evernham, crew chief for a three-time NASCAR Winston Cup champion

Racing Teams Demonstrate Good Teamwork Principles

Teams come in all shapes and sizes. While it's true that decisions are easier to make in a smaller team, a larger team has the opportunity for more creative problem solving based on a wider range of styles and perspectives. However, being small or large is not the issue; being the right size for the job is.

For example, racing teams consist of the driver and a seven-member pit crew who go over the wall on pit road to refuel the car and change the tires. Supporting this team, behind the wall, are the owner, crew chief, and garage mechanics. Each person is there because he or she brings knowledge and skills the team needs to achieve the overall vision.

In addition to being the right size for the job, racing teams practice good teamwork principles when they:

- Keep their eyes on the vision—the winner's circle—throughout the race

- Work together toward a common goal

- Develop a strong team identity

- Know the track and how to negotiate it

- Capitalize on a diverse array of talent and seek missing skills

- Maximize strengths and minimize weaknesses

- Use appropriate tools to get the car ready to race

- Follow the flags—a system of communication everyone understands

- Have a process in place—pitstops—for making on-the-spot repairs and adjustments

- Adjust their overall strategy at a moment's notice as conditions change and new information becomes available

- Celebrate when they take the checkered flag

- And finally, race again and again, constantly striving to improve over their last performance

Despite the obvious differences between the racetrack and the typical corporate environment, work-oriented teams need to do the same things racing teams do. For this reason, *Checkered Flag Teams* uses examples of teamwork in the racing world to illustrate what teamwork in the business world can be. If businesses were to apply proven team-building techniques like those in this book on a consistent basis, would these teams achieve checkered flag results?

We think so. The following interview will tell you why.

Renée Races Around the Track

As a team-building consultant, Renée Merchant often uses the metaphor of the race track to coach her clients on the principles of teamwork. The business people she works with can easily see the value of teamwork in racing. They can also understand how to apply their skills to building their own teams and achieving checkered flag results.

When asked why she uses the racetrack as a metaphor, she says, "I'd like to share with you one of the peak experiences of my life. My husband, Dick, gave me a very special present—a *Track Time* Driving School experience. I got to do what I enjoy watching race drivers do on summer Sunday afternoons. Just imagine . . .

I'm dressed in a heavy fire-resistant suit and gloves, and a cumbersome helmet restricts my peripheral vision. The butterflies in my stomach are dancing as I walk through the tunnel out to the pit. A row of stock cars waits gleaming in the sun. I climb through the window into "my" car, the Miller Lite number 2 Ford once driven by Rusty Wallace. Dean Daugharthy, my Track Time driving school instructor, straps me into the ill-fitting seat. I get into position—left hand on the steering wheel, right hand on the gearshift, left foot on the clutch, and right foot poised over the accelerator.

Dressed for driving, Renée Merchant climbs through the window of the Miller Lite number 2 Ford once driven by Rusty Wallace.

Dean reaches inside and flips the switch. VROOOM! The noise of the powerful engine surprises me. He shouts into my helmeted ear, "Go, go, go!" Excited, I step on the accelerator, ease up on the clutch, shift!! I push the gearshift into first, second, third, and finally, fourth gear. Out of the pit lane I go, remembering to stay below the yellow line until past turn 2. I look for oncoming cars, hard to do with a racecar's limited visibility and tiny mirrors. I ease up onto the backstretch; and I move from one racetrack groove into the next.

Suddenly, the wall is there. I'm there. I think, "This is real." It may be my fantasy, but this is REAL! I'm driving a competition stock car at my favorite speedway.

As I approach the wall on the back straightaway, my classroom lesson and practice come back to me. Time to look for the point at turn 3. I'm there. Now I look down to the left toward the orange cone at the midpoint between turns 3 and 4. I head for it. I'm there. I look up for the marker after turn 4. I head for it. I'm there. I take a quick look at the flag stand—I see a green flag—I go! In seconds, I'm across the start/finish line and heading toward turn 1.

The wall at turn 1 looms high—higher than I remember from driving my own car earlier. I resist the temptation to let off the accelerator. I head for the wall. I'm there. I look down to the left for the cone between turns 1 and 2. When I reach the cone, I remember the instructor's words, "Look up for the mark in turn 2. Where you look is where *you will go." I look up, see the mark and head for it. I'm there. I've completed one lap of this famous high-banked oval in the beautiful Irish Hills of southeast Michigan.*

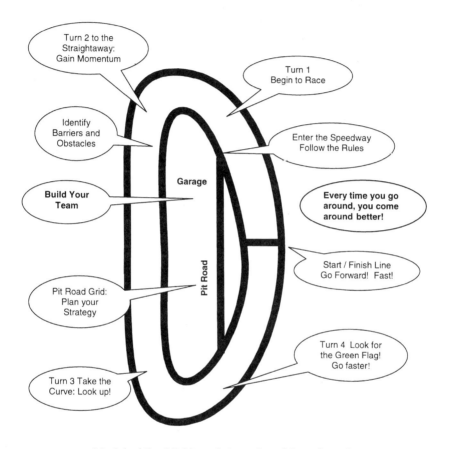

Model of the Michigan International Speedway in Brooklyn, Michigan: where you look is where you will go!

As I go around the track again and again, with every lap I try to improve my line and speed. Suddenly I realize I'm using the same words in my mind as I use in my team-building practice. "Every time we go around, we come around a little better.

This is the cycle of continuous improvement."
Wow! Stock car racing is like life. That insight is all
I have time for, because I'm at the next turn.

Soon, I feel almost comfortable with my speed
of 140 miles per hour. I relax to the point where I
can briefly look into the pits as I pass and see the
rest of my team. Yes, My Team. The instructors, the
fire crew, the ambulance crew and the track offi-
cials are all part of my team today. We have to-
gether shared a vision, clearly defined our
respective roles and responsibilities, and achieved
success. I realize that no stock car driver or busi-
ness leader can achieve anything without a team
ready to help in the pits or to offer support back at
the office. The synergy of real teamwork like I expe-
rienced today ensures checkered flag outcomes.

I take the white flag—one lap to finish, one last
chance to push myself to the limit. I take the check-
ered flag. I still have turns 1, 2, and 3. At the bot-
tom of turn 3, I slow to enter the pits, just as I've
seen my favorite drivers do hundreds of times.
When I stop, Dean helps me unbuckle and climb
out the window. "How was it?" he shouts. Over the
ringing in my ears, I shout back, "Incredible!"

I feel the same rush as I feel after a successful
training event or an effective performance improve-
ment outcome in my work. The feeling comes when
there's been real teamwork and the team has
achieved synergy. In my mind I see the words: "The
whole is greater than the sum of its parts." "To-
gether Everyone Achieves More." These are more
than mere platitudes hanging on colorful banners

in the workplace. I've driven a racecar—and I know. These words are true—and that's why car racing "speaks" to me—and to the teams I work with.

Fast Start Teamwork™ Tools Develop Synergy and Help a Team Take the Checkered Flag

In the workplace or at the racetrack, just putting a group of people together and calling them a team does not make them a team. Researcher Bob Kantor[*] describes it this way: "Teams are a higher form of organism than mere groups of individuals sharing information and tasks. They exist only after group members have made and demonstrated certain commitments to shared goals, visions, and values, and after they have articulated and reached consensus on roles, responsibilities, and processes."

Teams that develop synergy typically take the checkered flag, whatever the setting. These teams do not just happen by themselves. People need to take specific team-building actions with Fast Start Teamwork™ tools or other similar tools if they want to develop into a checkered flag team.

Work today is busy and demanding, and many people feel pressed for time. Busy managers and team leaders may look at the tools in this book and say to themselves, "I don't have time to do these things with my team. We need to get the job done."

---

[*] Director of Action Research Lotus Institute in Cambridge, Massachusetts

Yet if teamwork is a strategy your business is using to "drive productivity and results," then why not do it right?

The time that using the tools takes at the beginning *will save time in the long run*, because teams will avoid the problems and "potholes" that can so easily slow them down or throw them off the track entirely.

In addition to saving time and energy, Fast Start Teamwork™ tools have other advantages. They're simple and easy to use. Many of them are fun and good for a laugh or two. They help teams keep a balanced focus on both the task and the people side of team development. They ensure that the team benefits from everyone's ideas. Finally, they help team members "pack their bags" with transferable team skills they can take with them to their next team project.

What Kinds Of Teams Will Find This Book Useful?

Teams may be natural work groups organized around a process, customer, or physical location. An example of this kind of team is the Culture Change and Communications Team at a major utility. Teams like this one are ongoing and will do numerous projects together over time.

Teams may also be ad hoc, or project teams, formed to do a specific job. An example of an ad hoc team is the Process Education Team in the same utility. Members of such ad hoc teams may come from a single department, or they can be a cross-functional group. When they complete the work they have to do, ad hoc teams typically celebrate and disband.

Some people may be part of a natural work group team and simultaneously serve on one or more ad hoc teams.

Special teams are an intact group of highly skilled people who work well together and fulfill a specific function. Examples of special teams include transition teams that come into a business for a limited time between outgoing and incoming leaders; or crisis teams that take over temporarily during an emergency.

All of these kinds of teams can profitably use *Checkered Flag Teams*, whether they are start up teams, existing teams that have stalled, or teams stuck in conflict.

- **START UP TEAMS**—This new group of people beginning to work together need foundation tools to help them focus on their vision, work toward their goals, and master the interpersonal side of teamwork. This team will benefit most by starting with the first tool and working their way through to the last one. In this way, the tools become an integral part of their work.

- **STALLED TEAMS**—This team is in the middle of a work effort, and team members seem to get along well together. However, their performance has leveled off, and they've stopped moving toward achieving their vision. This team will benefit most from tools such as those that appear in the Data Flow and Problem Solving sections of the book (see chapters 6 and 7).

- **STUCK TEAMS**—Like a stalled team, this team is no longer making progress toward their vision. Interpersonal relationships have broken down as well, and people on this team are starting to avoid team meetings. Left to themselves, this team will most likely disband without completing their work. Team members need tools to help them manage conflict effectively and focus on their joint strengths instead of polarizing around their differences. Fast Start Teamwork™ Conflict Management tools (see Chapter 5) will help this team.

In summary, whatever your business, whatever state or stage your team is in, whatever type of team it is—if you're consulting with a team, leading a team, or contributing your time and talent as a team member, this book is written with you in mind.

laps to go!

CHAPTER

2

Building Knowledge

*"I think a lot about people, management, and psychology:
Specifically, how can I motivate my guys and make
them gel as a team? I surround them with ideas about
teamwork. I read every leadership book I can get
my hands on."*

—Ray Evernham, crew chief for a three-time Winston Cup champion

Knowledge Helps Build Synergy in Teams

Teams that develop synergy and take the checkered flag have
done their homework: They have the knowledge they need and
have prepared extensively. In a car race, for example, the driver
and the crew know the track, their own strengths and weaknesses, the car that will carry them to success, and the competition. They understand what's most important in teamwork,

15

and they put first things first. Finally, they understand the dynamics of teams.

Teams in the workplace face challenges similar to those of a racing team, though the challenges may go by different names. These teams, too, need extensive knowledge and preparation to succeed.

The Track

For any car race, the track is of paramount importance. It begins at the starting line and, ideally, ends in the winner's circle. Team members know its shape and length. They know the ultimate speed it will accommodate based on its turns and degree of banking. However, each day offers unique challenges. Recent rain, changing temperatures, sun, clouds, and previous use will affect track conditions. The team will assess the situation and make appropriate adjustments based on this data.

The "track" for a work team is their work environment in combination with the job they have to do. Like racing teams, business teams have a starting line and a vision to achieve. Often, a significant number of "laps" lies between the two. Racetracks typically don't have potholes, but the workplace often has symbolic equivalents of potholes for the team to avoid, such as poor communication or unclear expectations. Track conditions change instantaneously when an accident litters its surface with oil or debris. Similarly, sudden change in the workplace creates challenges for business teams. In times of change, knowledge and awareness can sometimes make the difference between failure and success.

Fast Start Teamwork™ tools a team can use to define their "track" include:

- Car Conversations, page 53
- Seeing the Championship Cup, page 58
- Tuning In to the Same Frequency, page 62
- Setting Milestones, page 84
- What's Driving This Car?, page 153
- Control/No Control, page 157

The Team

For winning a race, a high octane crew or team is essential. The race team includes not only the driver of the car, but also numerous others. The pit crew, the garage crew back home, the track officials, the safety crews, even the owners and fans—all of them contribute to the racing effort. Jeff Gordon, three-time Winston Cup champion, demonstrates the importance of the crew when he speaks of working to regain his position as a top contender in the NASCAR championship rankings. He says, "This new team is constantly gaining momentum and gaining confidence in one another."

People on a work team make it go. They're like the fuel in the car—and high octane is best! Others interested in the outcomes the team produces include shareholders, managers, suppliers and customers. The team's entire organization fills the "grandstand" and cheers the team on. Understanding the roles these various people play, being aware of how they interrelate, and knowing who has the power to clear the track of a trouble-some obstacle can be vital to a team as it pursues its goals.

Fast Start Teamwork™ tools a team can use to better understand their people include:

- What Kind of Car Are You?, page 44
- Getting Into the "Team Car," page 48
- CARStyles™ Inventory, page 67
- Do the Keys Fit the Locks?, page 90
- Team Billboard, page 92

The Car

A racecar is an awesome machine. The roar of its powerful engine and its brightly colored exterior covered with product names, logos and advertising slogans provide a large part of the racetrack ambience.

For the work team, the "car" may not be nearly so exciting, though it's equally necessary. The work team's car contains the team's strategy, processes, collective wisdom and energy, and collaborative spirit.

Fast Start Teamwork™ tools a team can use to know the "car" include:

- Rules for the Road, page 103
- Reducing Road Rage, page 105
- Take a Team Test Drive, page 116
- High Octane Teams, page 120
- The Loyal Fan, page 122

The Competition

The competition for a racing team consists of the other teams competing in the same race. The competition for a business team may be internal or external. Questions a business team may want to ask to take a look at their competition include the following:

- Is our vision aligned with the organization's vision?
- Do we have the resources we need?
- What stands in the way of our success?
- Are we willing to devote time to building our team?
- Are we willing to use conflict to our advantage?

The competition is always looking to catch an organization off guard. Able to respond only in the same old ways, the organization founders. A team may also founder when, for example, one team member takes credit for work another team member did, or when the boss announces that the team will have to finish the job with fewer resources. Team members need to *keep their team skills high* in order to respond creatively to situations like these.

Fast Start Teamwork™ tools a team can use to study the internal and external competition include:

Get a GRIP on the Wheel

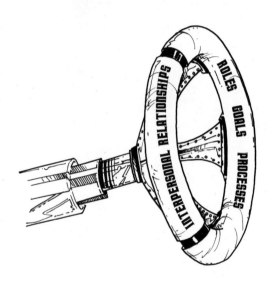

A working knowledge of the importance of some of the most critical factors that affect a team's success serves checkered flag teams well. GRIP is an acronym that covers four of these factors: Goals, Roles, Interpersonal Relationships and Processes. "Getting a GRIP on the Wheel" helps team members balance their priorities. With all due respect to those who developed the GRPI Model[*] (Goals, Roles, Processes, Interpersonal Relationships) that emphasizes the *order* of importance, our experience shows that keeping a balanced focus that includes interpersonal relationships builds teams faster and better.

---

[*] Michael Brimm, Ram Charan, Dale Lake, Hirotaka Takeuchi, and Noel Tichy developed this model in 1988.

Goals

The "G" in GRIP stands for Goals, sometimes called milestones. The process of forming goals begins with defining the mission. The mission tells a team how they're going to achieve the vision and identifies the starting line. Next, the team creates their vision—by describing the end-state results they want to achieve. Finally, the team determines goals that move them toward the vision.

Why are goals so important? Harold J. Leavitt and Jean Lipman-Blumen, co-authors of *Hot Groups*, have spent 20 years exploring why some teams do better than others. Effective groups "tend to grow around their task," says Lipman-Blumen " . . . it's the contributions that people make to a task that lead other people to respect them, to like them, to want to be around them. When people see someone bring something important to a task, they get excited about that."

Teams do best with the right number of goals—enough that they are challenged, not so many that they feel overwhelmed.

Short-Term and Long-Term Goals

Both short-term and long-term goals are important. In auto racing, the short-term goal is to win the next race, while the long-term goal or vision is to win the season championship. In the workplace, the organization using teams as a business strategy achieves its larger goal because teams achieve short-term goals along the way. Successful teams align the work they do with organizational vision and purpose.

FIGURE 1: Goals in Alignment

In much the same way, people come to work and participate on teams to achieve both their work goals and their personal and family goals. When personal goals are not congruent with professional and organizational goals, a person feels internal conflict. Sometimes this conflict is great enough to cause him or her to leave the team or even the organization.

In auto racing, people often change or leave teams during what's known as the "silly season." In the fall, race teams, sponsors, drivers, crew chiefs, and pit crew members start looking toward the next season. They sometimes find that they can no longer achieve their personal goals by participating on the team, just as people in the workplace do.

For example, a sponsor wants its car and advertising to be visible the greatest amount of time possible. Joyce Julius and Associates of Ann Arbor, Michigan, measures track advertising exposure for each race. Numerous statisticians and monitors tuned to the same race tally the number of times a sponsor's name is broadcast, and then they calculate the dollar value of this on-air time. If the team doesn't complete the race and records a DNF

(Did Not Finish), the on-air time is shorter, and the sponsor doesn't achieve its goal. As a result, the sponsor may decide to look for another driver or team. During the silly season, rumors fly about such potential changes. Some teams lose members at this time, but most remain intact and work toward achieving the season's goal until the year-end Championship banquet.

Being committed to team goals is one of the most important factors for a successful team. According to Dr. Greg Huszczo, management professor in the College of Business at Eastern Michigan University, "Goals define the very reason for a team to exist. They provide the team with purpose and sense of direction. Perhaps no other component of team effectiveness is as important."

Roles

The "R" in GRIP stands for Roles. In all teams, defining the roles each person plays is critical. In race teams, the owner, sponsor, driver, crew chief, car chief, and pit crew all have a role to play. If they have the knowledge and skills they need, the team is much more likely to succeed.

Business teams consist of similar stakeholder roles. These can include a champion, a team leader, team members, resource people with specific knowledge or information, and support people. Suppliers and customers partner with the team as well. All of these stakeholders expect to achieve their personal and professional goals by interacting with the team. As long as each one fulfills the expectations of his or her role, the team can expect to achieve its goals.

Tommy Cameron, Director for Public Relations for Michigan International Speedway, told this story about the importance of people understanding roles and responsibilities: "One of the greatest things I saw was when Phil Parsons was driving for the Melling Team at Daytona. There was a bad accident in turn 4. Six cars had spun. His spotter called on the radio, 'Pit lane. Pit lane.' Phil went down onto pit lane and was able to avoid the accident. The role of the spotter as part of the communication team was key to this positive outcome."

Interpersonal Relationships

The "I" in GRIP stands for Interpersonal Relationships. Ned Jarrett, two-time Winston Cup champion, says, "Everything comes down to the people business, and having the right people in the right place at the right time." *Fast Company* notes, "processes don't do work, people do." Having the right people for the job is vital. So is managing conflict between team members. When not used to the team's advantage, such conflict can lead to poor team performance or even outright failure.

Competition between team members can also get a team off track. People playing politics, protecting their turf, or jockeying for position can wreak havoc on a team's performance. As Ned Jarrett says, "Teams work best when everyone is pulling in the same direction toward a common goal."

CARStyles™, described in Chapter 4, or a similar personality typing instrument, helps team members understand different styles of interacting, learning, handling conflict, and solving problems. Although team members do not have to be close personal friends, they need to respect the strengths each person brings to the team if they want the team to succeed.

RACING WISDOM

Dean Daugharthy, Track Time™ instructor, described the importance of interpersonal relationships succinctly. When asked, "What one characteristic makes teams successful?" he responded, "People, their attitude and effort. If a guy has a bug in his pants, it affects everyone else, whether he's your best buddy or not."

WISDOM FROM ANOTHER RACING WORLD

Team EcoInternet participates in the sport of adventure racing. The sport combines hiking, biking, paddling, climbing and running through wilderness. A team of four or five athletes might race across the Australian Outback or the Sahara Desert, with no more than a compass, a map, and their experience and wits to guide them. Team member Robyn Benincasa says that unlike other teams she's raced with, EcoInternet doesn't waste time with internal competition. "All of us are of one mind—one mind with 10 arms and 10 legs. And that really makes a difference."

Processes

Finally, the "P" in GRIP stands for processes. For example, using processes the team has agreed upon and practiced when no conflict was present (see Chapter 5) can make managing conflict easier. A structured problem-solving process everyone understands and can use facilitates effective problem solving and decision making (see Chapter 7). These processes can make the difference between a DNF (Did Not Finish) team and one that completes the run and takes the checkered flag.

The key phrase is "agreed upon." Teams achieve the best results when team members create the team rules. Developing guidelines, or *Rules for the Road,* (see page 103) helps team members agree on processes and gives them a standard for measuring success.

Balance Is the Key

In today's competitive and fast-paced world, teams can easily get off-balance. They may focus exclusively on the task they have to do and neglect the "soft" or *people* side of team development. Then the people issues and the difficulty they can cause take them by surprise. Or perhaps they focus too heavily on the people side of teamwork and never get around to accomplishing their vision.

Focusing on both task and social aspects of team building simultaneously makes the "team car" go faster. Taking time for both in every team meeting is one option. Another is to have periodic off-site team-building days. Still another option is to concentrate on interpersonal relationships at first, and then, while focusing on the task, occasionally review or practice an interpersonal skill.

In short, successful teams maintain a *balanced* focus.

laps to go!

3

Understanding the Dynamics of Teams

"We talk about it all the time in the sport—Chemistry. And I think that's true in any business. Whether you're in a sport or in business, as long as you have people involved that have to depend on each other, if you don't have the right combination, you won't be successful."

—Ned Jarrett, NASCAR Winston Cup champion

Stages of Team Development

All teams share certain characteristics and go through predictable stages as team members develop interpersonal relationships and learn to work together effectively. These stages demonstrate what is sometimes referred to as the "orming" model developed by Bruce W. Tuckman (1965). The model includes the stages of forming, storming, norming, performing and adjourning. Tuckman used *adjourning* as the fifth stage for project teams that have completed their work and disbanded. We prefer to use the word "transforming."

Substituting "transforming" communicates three factors:

1. If the team is a project team (ad hoc or temporary), when they disband they help *transform* the culture and skill level of the organization by applying their new skills in future projects and sharing what they learned with others.
2. Intact work teams can help *transform* the organization and its product or service by seeking continuous improvement every day they continue to work together.
3. People from different departments who have worked on a team together may continue to interface with each other, build bridges that link departments, and *transform* the organization.

A Direct Relationship

During each stage of team development, the team faces certain tasks. Typically a team's effectiveness and performance develop in direct relationship with the rate and manner in which the team masters the tasks of each stage, as shown in the figure below.

Stages of Team Development—A Direct Relationship*

**Interpersonal
Social Relations**

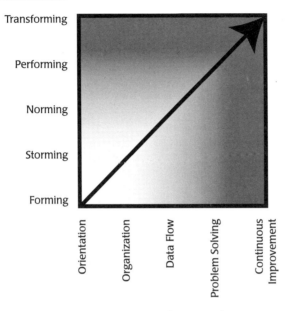

Task/Technical Functions

Fully functioning teams will focus on both task/technical
functions and interpersonal relationships.

Both Task and Social Aspects of Teamwork Matter

On the Y-axis of the Direct Relationship model are the "orming" phases—the social side of teamwork. On the X-axis are
the Task or Technical Functions—the team's job. The task side

---

* Developed by Delta Systems

of teamwork develops in direct relationship to the social stages on the Y-axis. This model makes it clear that a team cannot afford to neglect either the interpersonal/social side of teamwork or the task/technical side. Only with a balanced emphasis on both components of teamwork can a team reach its maximum potential. Each stage of building a team and the interpersonal tasks that go with it are described in more detail below.

FIGURE 3: Forming/Orientation

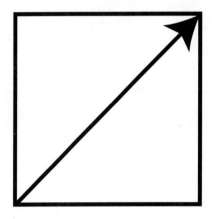

During the Forming/ Orientation stage, the team is at the starting line waiting for the green flag to wave.

Each team begins with Forming on the social side of the graph in Figure 3 and Orientation on the task side. At this point, the team is at the starting line waiting for the green flag to wave. Team members are beginning to ask questions: What are we about? What is the task we are to accomplish? What are we here for? Their tasks at this point are to:

- Get acquainted
- Focus their energy on building this team
- Agree on their mission and define the starting line
- Create and share a vision

- Learn more about each other's work style and preferences for assignments

Many team development books include agreeing on ground rules as a task for the Forming/Orientation stage. We prefer to do this task in the Storming/Organization stage when some difficulties have begun to appear. Laying ground rules at the beginning is often ineffective. People agree on common, ordinary courtesies easily but often don't think through how they're going to deal with a person who doesn't cooperate. If a problem has already occurred, people are upset. They tend to take the ground rules more seriously from that point on.

FIGURE 4: Storming/Organization

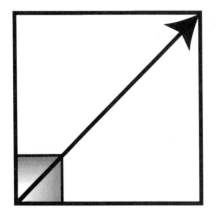

During the Storming/ Organization stage, the "team car" may sputter and backfire, or even stall. Some teams stop at this point because team members mistakenly conclude they cannot work together.

As the team begins to gather information and become more organized, team members may disagree on the goals and how to achieve them. Their different styles may throw them off track. Their "team car" may sputter and backfire, or even stall. Their questions are, "How on earth are we ever going to work together?" "What tools and processes do we need to use?" "Who's in charge here?" Some teams stop at this point because team members find it difficult to continue. People's feelings get hurt. Team members mistakenly conclude that they will never be able to work together.

If the team agrees to work through the Storming stage, putting interpersonal issues aside and focusing on task can help them move forward. Their tasks are to:

- Learn ways to encourage everyone's participation
- Set clear, challenging goals or milestones
- Match roles with responsibilities
- Create and strengthen a team identity
- Develop *Rules for the Road* (see page 103)
- Learn effective ways to manage conflict

FIGURE 5: Norming/Data Flow

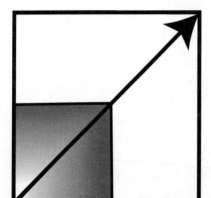

During the Norming/ Data Flow stage, information is flowing and the team car is picking up speed. Team members are learning to work well together and appreciate each other's differences.

In this stage of team development, information is flowing. The team car is picking up speed. Team members are aware of the skills and talent each of them brings to the team. Meeting arrangements and work procedures are routine. Team members appreciate each other's differences and are learning to work well together. Their tasks in this stage are to:

- Assess the team's potential
- Learn about the whole team's skills, talents, and strengths
- Appreciate the value of teamwork
- Reduce competition between team members or with other teams in the organization
- Add talent to the team if needed
- Anticipate change by keeping an eye on the environment

FIGURE 6: Performing/Problem Solving

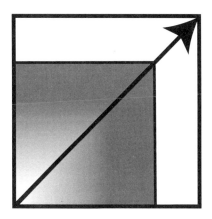

During the Performing/ Problem Solving stage, the team's car runs effortlessly and smoothly around the track, and the team most likely achieves success.

In this stage of team development, the team will learn how to approach new challenges and solve problems together effectively and efficiently. Their car runs effortlessly and smoothly around the track. The crew use their talents in ways that get the job done quickly and effectively. Humor and camaraderie are likely to be part of team meetings. Team members come to consensus easily. The team develops synergy—where the whole is greater than the sum of its parts. In this stage, their tasks are to:

- Learn problem-solving skills and use them
- Build consensus
- Remove obstacles to success
- Understand the team's scope
- Refocus on the vision and goals if needed
- Adjust their strategy as new information becomes available
- Celebrate success!

FIGURE 7: Transforming/Continuous Improvement

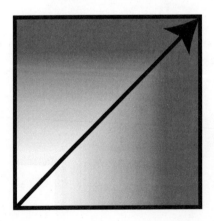

During the Transforming/ Continuous Improvement stage, the team either disbands or agrees to "go around the track" again. Either way, the team moves to a higher level of performance.

The team achieves the fifth stage of development *after* it has crossed the finish line and taken the checkered flag. With one job complete, the team either disbands or agrees to "go around the track" again. Either way, the team moves to a higher level of performance. Members of a fifth-stage team will usually perform better the second time around, either with this same team or with other teams. They can also share what they've learned with others. In these ways, they help the organization as a whole to perform better. Their tasks at this stage are to:

- Evaluate the team experience and identify what they've learned
- Share what they've learned with others
- Make changes in the team as required
- Make healthy transitions
- Start a new project at a higher level of performance

Getting Through the Stages of Team Development

Successful teams move *quickly* through the early laps of the team development race and on to the later stages that produce checkered flag results. The simple Fast Start Teamwork™ tools and activities shown in Figure 8 can help speed the team's journey.

In subsequent chapters, we will refer to the five stages of team development as follows:

1. Orientation
2. Organization
3. Data Flow
4. Problem Solving
5. Continuous Improvement

FIGURE 8: Steps Along the Pathway to the Checkered Flag, and Fast Start Teamwork™ Tools

Steps Along the Pathway to the Checkered Flag	Fast Start Teamwork™ Tools	Location in the Book
ORIENTATION		Chapter 4
Get acquainted	What Kind of Car Are You?	
Prepare for Teamwork	Getting into the "Team Car"	
Identify the team's mission and starting line	Car Conversations	
Create a vision	Seeing the Championship Cup	
Share the vision	Tuning In to the Same Frequency	
Learn about each other's work role, style and preferences for assignments	CARStyles™ Inventory	
ORGANIZATION		Chapter 5
Seek input from every team member	Gathering Collective Wisdom	
Set team goals	Setting Milestones	
Match roles and responsibilities to achieve goals	Do the Keys Fit the Locks?	
Create a team identity	Team Billboard	
Strengthen the team's identity	Visual and Verbal Team Symbols	
Set ground rules and/ or establish core values	Rules for the Road	
Learn effective ways to deal with conflict	Reducing Road Rage	

Steps Along the Pathway to the Checkered Flag	Fast Start Teamwork™ Tools	Location in the Book
DATA FLOW		Chapter 6
Assess the team's potential	Take a Team Test Drive	
Learn about each others' strengths, talents, skills and preferences	High Octane Teams or The Loyal Fan	
Appreciate the value of teamwork	The Auto Parts Store Challenge	
Reduce competition between team members or between teams	Go as Far as You Can	
Add talent to the team if needed	CARStyles™ Inventory, revisited	
Scan the environment	News from the Racetrack and the World	
PROBLEM SOLVING		Chapter 7
Learn problem-solving skills and use them	**FAST**™ Problem Solving	
Learn how to build consensus	We're In This Car Together	
Clear obstacles to success	What's Driving This Car?	
Understand scope	Control/No Control	
Measure team cohesion	Take a Team Test Drive, *Revisited*	
Refocus on the vision if needed	How Many Laps to Go?	
Adjust the strategy	Two Tires or Four?	
Celebrate!	Let the Driver Decide	

Steps Along the Pathway to the Checkered Flag	Fast Start Teamwork™ Tools	Location in this Chapter
CONTINUOUS IMPROVEMENT		Chapter 8
Evaluate the team's experience and identify what they've learned	Time for a Tune-up	
Share what they've learned with the organization	Spread-the-Word Checklist	
Make changes in the team as required	CARStyles™ Inventory *Revisited*; and Shifting Gears	
Start a new project at a higher level of performance	What Kind of Car Are You? (Go back to the Forming/ Orientation Stage)	

laps to go!

Running the Teamwork Race

The Green Flag Means "Go!"

Orientation–
Looking Toward
the Winner's Circle

"Where you look is where you will go."

—Dean Daugharthy, Track Time Trainer, instructing lay
students on how to negotiate a racetrack

FIGURE 9: A Guide to Chapter 4–Orientation

Steps Along the Pathway to the Checkered Flag	Fast Start Teamwork™ Tools	Location in this Chapter
Get acquainted	What Kind of Car Are You?	Page 44
Prepare for teamwork	Getting into the "Team Car"	Page 48
Identify the team's mission and starting line	Car Conversations	Page 53
Create a vision	Seeing the Championship Cup	Page 58
Share the vision	Tuning In to the Same Frequency	Page 62
Learn about each other's work role, style and preferences for assignments	CARStyles™ Inventory	Page 67

Getting Ready for the "Teamwork Race"

In the Orientation stage of building a team, team members prepare themselves and the systems in which they work for the journey ahead. A good first step on the journey toward the checkered flag is to get acquainted with teammates who may be strangers. The Fast Start Teamwork™ tool below, *What Kind of Car Are You?*, is an icebreaker. It helps a team begin or deepen the process of getting acquainted.

What Kind of Car Are You?

Materials

- Flip chart
- Markers

Procedure

1. The team leader or facilitator writes on flip chart paper the word "Introductions," and follows that heading with these sub-topics:
   - Name and Position?
   - From your perspective, what does this team do?
   - One or more questions that will elicit unique responses. Samples include:

—What can you tell us about yourself that no one in this room knows?

—If you were a car, what kind of vehicle would you be and why?

2. Going around the room, each person introduces himself or herself by answering the questions.

3. The team leader or facilitator may want to write on the flip chart the various answers team members give to the question, "What does this team do?"

Time Required

15–20 minutes depending on the size of group.

Tips for Best Use

- The team may want to use *What Kind of Car Are You?* in conjunction with the check in that follows.

- This first meeting sets the tone for future meetings. Time to have some fun!

Expected Results

People will have an opportunity to set aside the work they just came from and to learn surprising facts about new teammates. They'll get a good laugh or two and leave the meeting feeling good about participating on this team. The team leader or facilitator has gained valuable information that describes what the team does. He or she can use this information later when helping team members agree on their mission.

A Real-Life Story About Getting Acquainted

The staff of a law office met off-site to become better acquainted and work on some process improvement issues. The
team included two attorneys, an office manager, and two staff
people who performed research, typing and reception duties.
To begin the meeting, they used *What Kind of Car Are You?* as
an icebreaker. The question they used was, "What can you tell
us about yourself that no one in this room knows?"

Two of the women felt they knew each other very well and
would learn nothing new. One of the women surprised the
team when she announced that she played a musical instrument. The team discovered that each person in the office
played a different musical instrument, and together, they made
up a five-piece musical group. While they never actually
formed the group, their friendly discussion about the possibil-
ity of doing so led to more openness in the workplace. Greater
openness cleared the way for the team to improve their
processes.

Getting in the "Team Car"
Sets the Stage for Teamwork

Communication among team members occurs more readily
when team members are in the "team frame of mind." One
way to ensure that this team frame of mind happens is to reg-
ularly check in and check out of team meetings—in other
words, to climb into the team car. When they participate in
this simple activity, team members close the team car doors

Having fun imagining themselves as a five-piece musical group cleared
the way for this team to improve their processes.

and get ready to travel. They become separate from the rest of their often hectic work day and more able to focus on the work at hand.

Getting into the "Team Car" (Checking In)

Materials

- A talking object such as a talking stick, a stone, a Koosh™ ball—or a model car
- Face posters (optional)

Procedure

1. The first person holds the talking object and says a few words to describe his or her state of mind.
2. This person then says, "I'm in." Teammates can respond with the words, "You're welcome."
3. The person who spoke first passes the talking object to the next person who also enters the team car.
4. All members of the group check in, one by one, in this manner.
5. For the sake of speed, some teams prefer to use numbers to check in and out. Team members in turn announce a number to indicate where they are on the scale from 1 to 10. 1 = "I'm not really here today." 10 = "You have my full attention; I'm ready to participate."

6. Also for the sake of speed, the team leader or facilitator can focus the check-in process by asking a question such as, "What accomplishment from this past week are you most proud of?" Each person answers the question when it's his or her turn to speak.

7. Still another alternative is to post pictures from the Face Poster Check-In Kit of faces expressing different emotions. Team members can choose the poster that most closely expresses their mood and explain why.

Angry	Afraid	Sad
Cynical	Happy	Gung Ho

8. When it's time for the meeting to end, team members repeat the process to check out. Each one now has a chance to sum up feelings, share thoughts about the meeting, or respond to a cue such as, "What are you looking forward to?" After speaking, each one says, "I'm out," and passes the talking object to the next person. This process continues until each team member has had a chance to leave the meeting emotionally and get out of the team car.

See the order form at the back of the book to order the Face Poster Check-In Kit.

Time Required

Depending on the size of the group, from 2 to 7 minutes

Tips for Best Use

- Making check in and check out routine establishes an atmosphere in team meetings that team members will come to count on.
- The idea is to create a safe space for people. The person speaking can say whatever he or she wants to say or can pass if desired.
- Courtesy requires that no one else can speak while the person with the talking object is speaking.
- The team may want to set a talking time limit, particularly if experience on a particular team shows the need.

Expected Results

Team members will come to value this quiet time of entering and exiting the team car. The time provides a break between other parts of work and the team meeting and helps people focus on the work at hand. It also provides a way for team members to communicate how they're feeling to others if they want to. People have the opportunity to understand each other better and be more sensitive to other things going on in a person's life that may affect his or her behavior.

Caution Flag

In the hustle-bustle of the modern business world, some people will want to skip the check-in and check-out process. It will seem to them as though they are wasting time. It is our experience, however, that maintaining this practice helps keep the task and interpersonal sides of the team in balance.

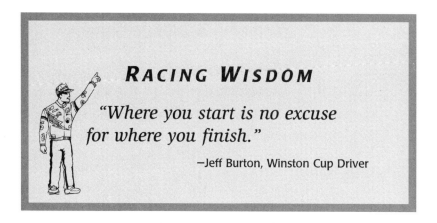

RACING WISDOM

"Where you start is no excuse for where you finish."

—Jeff Burton, Winston Cup Driver

The Mission Defines the Starting Line

The mission, sometimes called the purpose, is simply what the team does, who they do it for, and how they do it in order to achieve the results the organization wants. It describes the team's starting line. Sometimes, helping the team to agree to the mission can be quite a challenge for a team leader, facilitator or outside consultant.

People often get confused about the difference between a mission and a vision. The vision is future-oriented and represents what the team wants to be or create, while the mission represents what the team does *now*. However, both mission and vision are in present tense. Vision statements are in present tense because they describe the team's future *as if it were the present*. What a team says they are, they become.

In the NASCAR racing world, for example, the vision is to win the championship and take home the Winston Cup. The mission is to have the best car, driver and team possible in order to win races along the way to the championship.

This business example from Ford Commercial Truck Marketing and Sales also shows the distinction between the mission and the vision:

> **MISSION:** As a major supplier of commercial trucks, we provide knowledgeable professionals with the resources to lead in customer satisfaction.

> **VISION:** With our partners, we are the leading provider of commercial truck transportation solutions.

Car Conversations (Agreeing to the Mission)

Materials

- Copies of existing company or department published documents or advertising brochures
- Flip chart paper
- Markers
- Masking tape
- Copies of team members' responses to the question, "What Does This Team Do?" from the icebreaker (optional)

Procedure

1. The team leader or facilitator draws a large triangle on a piece of flip chart paper. At each point of the triangle, he or she writes one of the following three phrases: "What we do," "Who we do it for," and "How we do it."
2. Team members brainstorm one- or two-word descriptions of the team as it exists now for each of these headings.
3. The facilitator or team leader records these descriptions on flip chart paper, writing the ideas near the point of the triangle they describe as people call them out.
4. The team works together to select those items that are most descriptive of what they do *now* from the flip chart list and convert these ideas into a mission statement.

Time Required

45–60 minutes

Tips for Best Use

- The team needs to determine its mission at the beginning of the Orientation stage of team development.

- Sticky notes also work well as team members may need to move them from one point of the triangle to another.

- A start-up team will describe the purpose they believe is true.

- Team members need to stay focused on the "now," not the future.

- The team can display the mission in the work area near the display of the vision they will create next.

Expected Results

The mission is the starting line for the checkered flag team. The team begins wherever they are. Focusing on "now" in this way avoids bringing up history or negative experiences, and prevents people from turning the meeting into a gripe session.

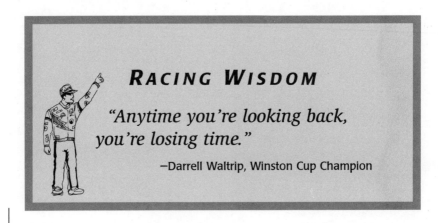

RACING WISDOM

"Anytime you're looking back, you're losing time."

–Darrell Waltrip, Winston Cup Champion

Creating the Vision

Racecar owners form teams to run the best race they possibly can and to cross the finish line first. Business leaders form teams for a business reason, such as to increase quality, reduce waste, or improve a process. Teams in either setting have a specific job to do and know what they must accomplish.

Knowing what they must accomplish is not the same as having a vision. The question for the team is, "What will success look like?" That desired state of affairs is the vision, and the team's next task is to articulate it. The vision of a racing team might be, "We will stand in the Winner's Circle and receive the trophy for the Winston Cup championship." They achieve this long-term vision by achieving short-term goals or milestones—winning races.

Just as a car drives better when the tires are aligned, a team—and the organization it's part of—do better when the team's vision is aligned with the organization's vision. A top priority of the vision—the collective view of the team's preferred future—is that everyone involved wins. The best visions also help team members achieve their individual goals and motivate them to participate enthusiastically in the team's work.

Examples of Visions

Teams can write their visions in a variety of styles. Some vision statements are short and simple to remember, such as these two:

Leadership team of a third-tier* Automotive Manufacturer:

Committed to always "do the right thing"—for our customers, employees, suppliers, owners and community.

Training Department in a Power Plant:

We are the industry leader in facilitating customers' success by providing cost-effective performance solutions.

Or, visions may be longer, as the following demonstrate:

Quality Department, Automotive Supplier:

We are a highly motivated, solutions-oriented Team committed to problem analysis and prevention for both our internal and external customers. We are dedicated to exceeding customer expectations by becoming the Global Industry Leader in Quality Assurance through Continuous Improvement.

Financial Controls Department of a Utility:

We are a high performance team partnering with our customers by being a premier provider of financial information, alternatives and solutions. Some see numbers, we see opportunities.

Maintenance Department of a Utility:

We are a valuable resource for our Company with our experience and service capability. We provide dependable,

---

* The tier system is common in the automotive industry today. In this system, each level of suppliers in the supply chain hierarchy manages the suppliers at the next lower level.

knowledgeable expertise to help others work safely and reliably. We provide leadership to train others and add value for the Company, plant and shareholders.

Automotive Supplier, Joint Union-Management Team:

We take pride in our commitment to working together to create the ideal working environment and to be recognized by our Customers as the Industry Leader in Quality, Productivity, and Technology.

Common Threads
Run Through the Visions

Common threads run through these vision statements. All the organizations that created them are using teams as a business strategy. The visions include such things as putting customers first, partnering with others, and focusing on quality and leadership. In each of the above examples, the team working together with the team leader generated the vision statement:

- In the case of the power plant, 30 people representing the union, management and staff worked together to create their vision statement.
- In the case of the maintenance department, some employees had to remain on duty at all times. The outside consultant divided the department in half and met with each half separately to implement the Fast Start Teamwork™ process in a series of meetings.

This approach allowed the other half of the team to provide needed support to the plant. The consultant displayed the two separately generated visions on flip chart paper, and in subsequent department meetings, the whole team merged the two statements into one vision. The unusual method worked because the department manager was committed to making teamwork their way of work life.

Seeing the Championship Cup (Creating a Vision)

Materials

- Copies of the company's vision statement and other published company materials
- Copy of the team's mission statement
- Examples of well-written vision statements from other companies or teams
- 5″ × 8″ cards in various colors
- Markers
- Masking tape

Procedure

1. The team leader or facilitator posts the company's vision and other published material so team members can easily see it.

2. The group may want to spend some time talking about the company's vision and how they think the job their team is charged with relates to and supports it.

3. The team leader or facilitator poses the questions, "If we do what we're supposed to do as a team, what will success look like?" And, "Who will we be?

4. Team members answer these questions individually, writing one idea on each card.

5. They post their ideas on the wall.

6. Team members take a few minutes to discuss the ideas with each other. Working together, they group the ideas into clusters. Natural groupings will usually occur.

7. Working with the team leader or facilitator, the team members write a vision that incorporates all the major ideas that emerged in the brainstorming* session.

Time Required

2–3 hours

Tips for Best Use

- A broad variety of vision statements to use as models will give the team some good ideas.

- This activity may work better if done in two sessions—the first for brainstorming; the second, for creating the actual vision statement. During the in-

---

* Brainstorming is a technique teams often use to generate ideas. Team members suggest as many ideas as they can, and no one judges any idea at this point.

tervening time, team members can think about the ideas that came up in the brainstorming session.

- Sticky notes are a good substitute for cards for this activity.

Expected Results

Once they have created a vision statement that pleases them, the team will typically want to reproduce the vision and display it on posters, the backs of business cards, and advertising brochures. The plant team mentioned above had large signs produced in time for the first open house they had held in a long time. They wanted to showcase their work for their families and community to see.

Caution Flag

It's relatively easy to craft a lofty vision statement that sounds great and motivates no one. It's far more difficult to write a concise, compelling vision that touches people's minds and hearts. Successful teams take the time to write the "right" vision.

A Real-Life Example of Creating a Vision

The two partners of a home health care service company wanted to create a vision the entire company of about 40 home health aides would support. The problem was that the aides got their assignments mostly over the telephone and did not meet as a group. The partners worked with their advisory board to draft a vision statement. They reproduced the vision statement on very large flip chart paper and posted it in the office area. At the end of the month, when all the aides reported in person to receive their paychecks, they were able to study the vision statement and write comments, additions, and changes. The following week the partners finalized the vision statement using the input from staff. They then printed and distributed the statement for all to see. This process worked very well in unifying an otherwise physically scattered work team. People were ready to commit to achieving the vision because they had participated in creating it.

Team members pair up to explain their
understanding of the vision.

Sharing the Vision

Successful teams have a shared vision.

The team has just spent several hours creating the vision. Doesn't this mean that it is already shared? Not necessarily, because each person may have a different interpretation of the words themselves. They need to work together to actively share their vision.

Peter Senge says in *The Fifth Discipline*, "A shared vision is not an idea. It is, rather, a force in people's hearts, a force of impressive power. It may be inspired by an idea, but once it goes further—if it is compelling enough to acquire the support of more than one person—then it is no longer an abstraction . . . People begin to see it as if it exists. Few, if any, forces in human affairs are as powerful as shared vision."

Shared vision is not an easy thing to build, nor is the process of sharing the vision ever completely done. Developing and maintaining a shared vision is an ongoing process. The power of the vision comes from the fact that it's alive. When the team continually talks about it, it becomes *the way,* a guiding force in how people behave and in what they aspire to do.

Tuning in to the Same Frequency (Sharing the Vision)*

Materials

- 5" × 8" cards
- Pens of various colors

---

* Based on a Shared Vision exercise done by Chuck Roe & Associates, Inc., for Worldwide Customer Day for Philips Electronics. Used with permission.

Procedure

1. Each team member writes his or her understanding of the vision the team has created on a card, without necessarily using the exact words of the vision. What does it mean to each individual? How does it fit in with or align with the person's individual goals?
2. Each team member then pairs up with another team member.
3. One member of each pair talks to the other member of the pair for approximately two minutes, explaining his or her understanding of the vision to the teammate, using examples, describing what the final result will look and feel like, and particularly relating the team vision to his or her personal vision.
4. Then the other member of the pair shares his or her perceptions by responding to the same questions.
5. Team members then switch partners and repeat the vision-sharing process.
6. They continue switching partners and talking to each other through three rounds of sharing.
7. Team members come back together and debrief the rest of the team on their experience.

Time Required

30 minutes, plus 10–15 minutes for debriefing

Tips for Best Use

- Team members will benefit more from this exercise if they listen respectfully to others and ask questions for further understanding of other perspectives.

- A fun alternative is for team members to draw their understanding of the vision and explain their pictures to one another.

- Still another alternative is for team members to bring in an object or a picture that portrays the vision for them. In the sharing sessions, they can explain why the item they bring represents the vision.

- It is helpful for team members to look for commonalties as they talk with one another.

Expected Results

Team members will come closer to having a common vision as they do this exercise together. They will also learn more about each other. They will begin to think about how their personal vision aligns with the team's vision. If they find misalignment, now is the time to address this problem to encourage team synergy.

Many teams come to this activity thinking they are miles apart—and they are energized to discover how closely aligned they actually are. If teams find themselves polarized and in sharp disagreement, they have a couple of opportunities. They can possibly expand their vision or modify it. Or perhaps they'll decide to form two sub-teams to work on different parts of the vision or approach it from two different perspectives. Either way, they deal with the polarity rather than pretending it doesn't exist. Successful teams work through their differences and find creative solutions.

Caution Flag

For best results, team members will want to approach this exercise thoughtfully, and make a serious effort to connect the team's vision to their own personal goals. They will also want to listen respectfully to their teammates and inquire for a deeper understanding. They will want to avoid getting stalled in debate and using the vision as a way to complain about the past.

A Real-Life Story About Sharing the Vision

An outside consultant gave team members the following assignment: Bring in a picture (from a magazine or one you draw) that represents this team's vision to you. One team member drew his picture on flip chart paper. It was a sailboat, surrounded by water and clouds, obviously moving with a brisk wind. A stick figure at the tiller was steering, but the boat had no rudder. He explained, "Sometimes I feel like this plant is a rudderless boat with no real sense of direction. The wind just blows us around."

His picture and comment were eye-openers for the team as a whole. They realized that they needed a clear vision to provide needed direction and would most likely not achieve their goals without it.

Learning About Each Other's Work Styles and Preferences for Work Assignments

One of the most common reasons teams fail to develop synergy is a lack of understanding about team members' communication styles and preferences for solving problems or managing conflict. People are by nature and experiences different in all sorts of ways, and each of these ways may affect how each person approaches a job and how he or she communicates. When two people who are opposites in some ways become members of the same team, they can easily misjudge one another when these differences emerge. The push-pull dynamic that occurs when two members or factions of a team war against each other rather than pulling together can at best slow the team down considerably or at worst stop their progress altogether.

Numerous tools exist to help team members learn that others aren't "wrong" just because they're different. Several of these, such as DISC, Wilson, and True Colors, rely on dividing people into four types. Experience shows that teams have a greater capacity to do better work if they have members from all four types or quadrants.

One such self-assessment tool, CARStyles™ Inventory*, capitalizes on the fact that people often express their preferences by the car they prefer to drive. This inventory helps the team-to-be accomplish several vital tasks in a fun and memorable way:

- Getting better acquainted
- Learning about each other's different work and communication styles
- Learning how to adjust personal style to aid communication
- Providing a basis for suggesting changes for additional talent or knowledge the team needs

---

* Developed and distributed by Delta Systems.

CARStyles™ Inventory is based on four personality types that correspond to four automobile types. When people respond to the "getting acquainted" question, "If you were a car, what vehicle would you be?" they describe their car by what it means to them or does for them. When they do this, they're describing the characteristic behaviors of each personality type the inventory identifies:

- Utility Vehicle or Pick-Up Truck (see page 205)
- Full Size Sedan (see page 206)
- Sporty Coupe (see page 207)
- Minivan (see page 208)

CARStyles™ is a tool that is easy to understand and facilitate. It tends to be self-validating. Team members will easily remember their type and that of other team members. They can have a lot of fun with CARStyles™ and simultaneously learn useful information about themselves and their teammates.

CARStyles™ Inventory

Materials

- CARStyles™ Inventory Participant paired words self-assessment and matrix (see page 202)
- Flip chart
- Markers

See the order form at the back of the book to order CARStyles™ Participant Guide and Facilitator Guide with interpretation.

Procedure

1. Team members begin by completing the paired words portion of the questionnaire.

2. Working individually, they select from the pairings the word that best describes them at work *as a fellow worker views them*. The words are not opposites. While both words may be somewhat descriptive, one is typically more powerful than the other for the individual completing the questionnaire.

3. Each team member then totals the checked words at the bottom of the page and plots the two letters with the most checks on the matrix. People will fall into one of four quadrants:

     CA (Control-oriented and Ask-assertive)—
        utility vehicle

     CS (Control-oriented and State-assertive)—
        full size sedan

     RS (Relationship-oriented and State-assertive)—
        sporty coupe

     RA (Relationship-oriented and Ask-assertive)—
        minivan

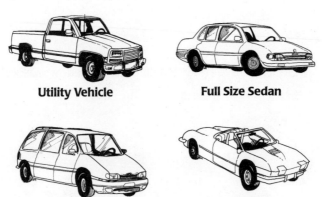

Utility Vehicle   **Full Size Sedan**

Minivan   **Sporty Coupe**

4. Once each team member has completed this task, the team will want to spend some time interpreting the results, either with the help of a facilitator or the use of the *Facilitator Guide*.

5. The facilitator then draws the Team Profile on flip chart paper. Typically, the team displays the Team Profile in the team work area as a reference, and as part of the Team Identity. The figure below shows a sample Team Profile.

Sample Team Profile

*Control-oriented

	UTILITY VEHICLE	FULL SIZE SEDAN	
*A s k a s s e r t i v e	Detail-oriented Proficient and Practical Systematic and Dependable **Pat**	Goal-oriented Candid and Dynamic Refined and Commanding **Sandy**	*S t a t e a s s e r t i v e
	MINIVAN	SPORTY COUPE	
	People and Team-oriented Steady and Inclusive Considerate and Supportive **Terry**	Idea-oriented Stylish and Spirited Enthusiastic and Imaginative **Gerry**	

*Relationship-oriented

A well-balanced team has members from all four CARStyles™ quadrants and benefits from a variety of perspectives.

Time Required

15 minutes for the self-assessment
One hour for interpretation and discussion of the results

Tips for Best Use

- It is most appropriate to use CARStyles™ early in the Orientation stage of team development, although it can be useful at any time.
- To improve understanding, team members can provide examples of working together that fit their profile or vary from it.
- It is a good idea to post the Team Profile in the work area for easy reference.
- After a new team member has been with the team a couple of weeks, the team leader or facilitator can provide the CARStyles™ Inventory self-assessment tool and add the new person to the Team Profile. Team members can coach the new member about the characteristics of the different styles.

Expected Results

Each team member will plot his or her own style on a Team Profile. The facilitator or team leader will explain the characteristics of each of the four styles. Immediately, team members begin to understand why they instantly found it easier or harder to relate to or understand another team member.

The major benefit of using the CARStyles™ Inventory is that it helps team members understand that people are innately different. They have different ways of communicating, different work styles, different perspectives of their roles, different ways of handling conflict, and different skills and talents. Successful teams learn to capitalize on these personality differences and develop strategies to improve communication between personality types.

Capitalizing on differences enhances the team's likelihood of success. For example, the analytical *Utility Vehicle* wants to gather lots of data before suggesting a solution—and can be counted on to provide an in-depth analysis of any situation. The opposite, the more expressive *Sporty Coupe,* will become impatient and jump to conclusions that seem correct from his or her perspective. While this behavior may not be good, the *Sporty Coupe* will provide lots of ideas and imagination to the team. The *Full Size Sedan* will announce the solution that makes sense to him or her, and help the team set goals and stay on track. The opposite, the congenial *Minivan*, will want to talk over coffee about how best to proceed. He or she is steady and inclusive, a real people person. In short, all types help the team achieve their goal; it is simply their way of doing it that differs.

Research has shown that groups with diverse membership may have more difficulty gelling as a team. However, if teams manage their diversity well, they tend to be more productive, have a higher level of creativity and innovation, and solve problems better. (Cox, 1993.) A diverse team that has learned to capitalize on its diversity is highly likely to develop synergy and take the checkered flag.

Caution Flags

CARStyles™ has nothing to do with the cost of a vehicle, socioeconomic standard of the individual, or whether the person actually owns or leases the particular vehicle. It relates only to communication style as described by the individual's behavior in relation to how that person perceives the features of various types of motor vehicles.

Some team members may get upset if they "test" differently from the car they drive. In this situation, the team leader or facilitator can emphasize that this typing instrument is not intended to be scientific, but rather to make the major point that people are different, and that a varied mix of people makes a better team.

Also, some people will not score in only one quadrant, but may be a blend of two. For example, a person may score 7 and 8 on the State-assertive side. He or she is probably displaying the communication style of both the *Full Size Sedan* and the *Sporty Coupe*. This driver/expresser type of person is a blend of goal and idea orientation. It is helpful for the team leader or facilitator to ask the question, "Under stress, what is your typical behavior?" If the person becomes rigid and tough, refusing to give an inch, he or she is probably a *Full Size Sedan*. If the person speaks faster, becomes loud and more outgoing, exploding like a bomb, he or she is probably a *Sporty Coupe*.

See the *CARStyles™ Facilitator Guide* for details and explanations of other blends.

laps to go!

5

Organization—Smoothing the Way, Gathering Speed

"You can have the fastest engine, most aggressive driver, and best-skilled pit crew, but if they ain't working together as a Team, you've got nothing."

—Richard Petty, NASCAR legend

FIGURE 10: A Guide to Chapter 5—Organization

Steps Along the Pathway to the Checkered Flag	Fast Start Teamwork™ Tools	Location in this Chapter
Seek input from every team member	Gathering Collective Wisdom	Page 74
Set team goals	Setting Milestones	Page 84
Match roles and responsibilities to achieve goals	Do the Keys Fit the Locks?	Page 90
Create a team identity	Team Billboard	Page 92
Strengthen the team's identity	Visual and Verbal Team Symbols	Page 98
Set ground rules and/or establish core values	Rules for the Road	Page 103
Learn effective ways to deal with conflict	Reducing Road Rage	Page 105

Gathering Collective Wisdom

Teams work better if *all* members share their skills, talents and wisdom. A flip chart is a tool that a team can use in a variety of ways to record and organize the team's collective wisdom. One common method of gathering this collective wisdom is brainstorming. Traditional brainstorming, described below, is excellent for gathering ideas, but it tends to appeal to the *Full Size Sedans* and *Sporty Coupes* on a team more than it does to *Utility Vehicles* and *Minivans*. A variation, "quiet brainstorming," uses cards or sticky notes instead of a flip chart and ensures that each team member has a voice.

Flip Charts

Materials

- An easel for holding flip chart pads
- Flip chart pads
- Markers of various colors, such as Mr. Sketch®
- Masking tape

Procedure

1. At any time during a team meeting, team members may need to share ideas through words or pictures. Flip chart paper and markers make this an easy task.
2. The team leader or facilitator can print the meeting agenda

Flip charts are wonderful when the team wants
to brainstorm some ideas.

on flip chart paper and post it where everyone can see it. This visual reminder makes it easier to stay on task.

3. The team can develop the agenda over time on a flip chart left in the team meeting room for that purpose. Throughout the week, as team members think of something they would like to present to the group, they can add it to the developing agenda.

4. The team can label one piece of flip chart paper "The Parking Lot." The team lists items they cannot immediately resolve on that sheet to explore at a more favorable time.

5. Flip charts are wonderful when the team wants to brainstorm some ideas. As team members call out ideas, one

team member or the facilitator can capture them on the paper for all to see.

6. Flip charts also work well for planning and prioritizing activities.

7. Flip chart paper makes it easy to display the problem-solving work that the team is doing, on successive sheets of paper attached to the wall. Using paper this way gives the team a constant resource to refer to when there is misunderstanding or disagreement or simply the need to check facts. After the meeting, the team may want to type the information on the flip charts and distribute it to team members. An alternative is to take pictures of the flip chart pages with a digital camera and keep permanent records in this manner.

8. When the team needs a break, they can grab a piece of flip chart paper and work together to make something out of it—a quick team-building project. Examples include the world's best paper airplane, or hats for everybody to represent different perspectives.

Time Required

None in addition to the team's regular work

Tips for Best Use

- Different team members can write on the flip charts on different days to spread the workload.
- The writer needs to verify that he or she has captured what the team said or did.
- The team can keep the flip chart sheets for future reference until they have completed their work.

Expected Results

The team will have an easy and reliable way to record what happens in team meetings, to think aloud together, and to plan future meetings. Because they have all seen the same ideas written down, they have a shared understanding of what has happened in the team process.

Caution Flag

It's easy to let flip chart sheets gather dust in a corner. Having the information on them readily available is most likely when one person takes responsibility for the sheets. That person can keep the sheets and hang them back on the wall at the next meeting. For documentation purposes, he or she can transcribe the information or take a picture of it using a digital camera, and then distribute it to all team members.

5″ × 8″ Cards

5″ × 8″ cards in various colors work well for quiet brainstorming. Different colors can indicate headings for groupings or can represent the answer to a specific question. For example, all answers to Q3 might be blue, while all responses to Q4 might be green.

Using stacks of cards, people brainstorm individually, writing one idea per card. Writing ideas in this way ensures that quiet team members can easily contribute. A team member or the facilitator tapes the cards to the wall. Team members can easily rearrange, group, and combine the cards, or they can remove one or more of them completely if the group determines they don't fit. When the activity is over, team members can

"Quiet Brainstorming" with 5" × 8" Cards

After the quiet brainstorming activity is over, people move to
the wall to read and discuss all the contributions.

easily number and stack the cards, either to store or to transcribe for distribution and future work.

Materials

- Packets of 5" × 8" cards in various colors

- Pens or markers

- Masking tape

- Flip chart

Procedure

1. The team leader or facilitator posts the overall goal or object of the activity on the wall or writes it on a flip chart.

2. If there are individual questions to which the team will respond, the team leader or facilitator can write the questions on a flip chart.

3. The team leader or facilitator gives each team member a stack of colored cards and a marker to record ideas—one item per card. Sticking to one color at a time is important for sorting ease.

4. As they record their ideas, team members can hand the card to the facilitator to post or post it themselves.

5. After the brainstorming activity is over (about seven minutes is optimal), people move to the wall to read and discuss all the contributions.

6. Team members work together to a) group the cards by commonality and b) combine duplicates. Logical groupings will typically emerge.

7. An alternative is for the team to divide into groups of two or three. Each group discusses the answers to a particular question and groups them. They then report back to the team why they made the choices they did.

8. Team members discuss the items and groupings. They may add new cards and discard inappropriate ones by team consensus.

9. A team member takes the responsibility to number the cards for easy placement at subsequent meetings, or to transcribe and distribute them.

Time required

None in addition to regular team meetings

Tips for Best Use

- Using cards in this way works well for planning a project, identifying mission, vision, and goals, matching responsibilities with roles, identifying problem sources, reflecting on past performance, and brainstorming continuous improvement possibilities.

- A large supply of cards in a variety of colors enables teams to use color-coding when appropriate.

- Team members may want to take turns posting their ideas, reading them aloud as they do so. Sometimes their words will spark ideas in others.

- Large sticky notes are an excellent alternative because they require no tape.

- Hexagon-shaped sticky notes work especially well when it is important for the team to see how things relate to one another.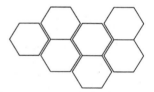

Expected Results

These "quiet brainstorming" options offer a great deal of flexibility and give all team members an easy way to contribute ideas. The different colors aid the team in sorting and grouping and are especially appealing to visually oriented people.

Caution Flag

Ideas can easily get lost. As with any form of brainstorming, it is important to keep a record of the ideas the activity generates. Ways to do this include one team member taking responsibility to transcribe and distribute the information, or to take pictures of the posted information with a digital camera and record it that way.

Setting Team Goals or Milestones

A team can use a flip chart, cards or sticky notes as they accomplish a number of vitally important team tasks. Setting goals or milestones is one of the most important of these tasks. Goals are the specific targets the team will set out to reach in order to support the mission and to achieve the vision team members have created together.

SMART Goals

Studies have shown that "good" goals have certain characteristics—in other words, they're S-M-A-R-T:

S pecific: they address specific opportunities and/or problems

M easureable: they contain an agreed-upon standard

A chievable: they challenge the team but are attainable

R elevant: they have a visible, positive effect on the team and company

T imely: they include clearly defined milestones and deadlines

Examples of SMART goals are:

- We will finish every race this season, and finish in the top 10 at least 50% of the time.

- We will improve our quality by 10% to 99% as measured by rejected parts by year end.

GAPs

The GAP concept (Goals, Action Steps, Performance) may also be helpful to think about when setting goals. Keeping their vision in mind, team members set the goals they need to achieve along the way, plan action steps to achieve these goals, and perform the action steps.

For example, the goal of a pitstop is to get the car back on the track faster than the competition. Ray Evernham noted that his pit crew can accomplish this goal in 17 seconds, one second less than other pit crews at the time of the measurement. During that one second, a racecar going 200 mph can travel approximately 300 feet, potentially putting the driver ahead of the competition. Tiny actions like this can create huge GAPs that will put the team out in front faster.

As in a race, when business teams achieve their goals, they close the gap between the team's starting line and the winner's circle.

Ray Evernham's pit crew can
accomplish the goal of getting the
car back on track in just 17 seconds.

Examples of Goal Statements

A joint union-management team was successful in identifying goal statements that tied their vision to specific goals. Over subsequent meetings, they identified and agreed to key result areas (KRA) and key indicators (KI) for each area along with a target (stretch goal). The KRA included Processes, Quality, Profitability, and Work Environment (safety and teamwork). An example is shown on the following page.

When a team has very specific goals such as these, measuring success is easy.

Key Result Area	Key Indicator	Target
Work Environment	Safety	Frequency 5.9 Severity 29 Incident Rate 22
Processes	Inventory Turns Productivity Index	22 < 1.08
Quality	Plant Delivery Performance Customer parts/million Process parts/million	100% 45 50 (10% reduction)
Profitability	Return on Investment	22%

Setting Milestones
(Establishing Team Goals)

Materials

- Copy of Vision, Mission, Key Result Areas, or whatever the team is tracking now
- 5" × 8" cards
- Markers
- Masking tape

Procedure

1. The team leader or facilitator posts the Vision, Mission, and Key Result Areas on the wall.
2. Team members brainstorm work areas/activities that they will have to improve in order to achieve the vision, writing one idea per card.

3. Team members sort these ideas into logical groups and create a title for each group, the goal or milestone heading. The team leader or facilitator can post the milestone headings on the wall. An example of a milestone heading is "Customer Satisfaction."

4. Team members move to the wall to sort the cards underneath the headings and agree to specific milestone statement components.

5. The team then divides into smaller groups of two or three, and each group takes one heading with all its component statements to write a SMART milestone statement.

Time Required

2–4 hours

The team may complete this activity in two or more separate meetings

Tips for Best Use

- Hexagon-shaped sticky notes work well as an alternative to cards for this exercise as they help team members see connections between milestone components.

- Milestone statements work best when worded positively. Negative goals, such as "Lose 30 pounds," or "Quit smoking" are difficult to achieve. A positive statement might be "Walk two miles three times a week."

- Each team member keeps a copy of the milestone statements to track his or her progress.

- Team members prepare individual milestones based on each team member's role in the team process.

- The team may want to post an enlarged copy of the milestone statements. An artistic person may want to post them on a picture of a road or racetrack and place it where team members can see it often.

- Marking off milestones that they have achieved gives the team an awareness of their accomplishments.

Expected Results

Team members set and commit to team goals or milestones together, thereby increasing ownership. Since they now have team goals, setting individual performance goals is easier. Having a copy of the team's goal statements also helps team members track their own progress. Having a large version of the goals posted will help the team see how their individual progress relates to and contributes to the team's progress.

Roles and Responsibilities

Once the team has identified their Mission, Vision, and Milestones, they will need to fill required roles. In a race team pit crew, for example, specific roles and responsibilities, skills and strengths help the team take the checkered flag. Many teams have lost races not on the racetrack, but in the pits, perhaps because the tire man didn't replace the lug nuts tightly. Or the crew chief calculated there was enough fuel to go the distance when there wasn't, because the gas handler didn't completely fill the tank.

In contrast, a top pit crew not only fulfills the responsibilities of their roles, but they constantly try to do it better. *Fortune* magazine describes them this way: " . . . seven men over the wall working on the car itself, another eight to ten on the other side handing them things and clearing away equipment—can change all four tires, [pump] 21 gallons of gas into the tank, clean the windshield, and give the driver a drink, all in under 20 seconds . . . These folks have checked their self-interest back in the garage somewhere and moved to another zone . . . they have created a collective ego, one that gets results unattainable by people merely working side by side."

In workplace teams, there are specific known roles to fill that, as in a race, depend on each other. These can include the following:

- The *champion* is a management team member who agrees to support the team's efforts. He or she generally has a particular interest in the outcome. The champion ensures that appropriate resources are available for the team and helps to remove obstacles to success.

- The *team leader* is usually an equal member of the team with extra duties to perform. The team can fill this position in a number of ways:

  —By appointing someone based on specific criteria

  —By a member volunteering

  —By team agreement

Voting to fill the team leader role is not a good choice, because the process of voting creates winners and losers. Winners and losers cannot exist on the same team. Even when management has allowed a "secret" ballot to take place, those who voted against the selected team leader know they "lost" and have an excuse for not supporting the team leader and team decisions.

The team leader role includes the responsibilities of handling administrative functions; interfacing with management, suppliers, and customers; facilitating team meetings; keeping the vision alive; identifying and securing resources; and cheerleading for the team. The team leader needs the patience to share information, the trust to let others make decisions, and the ability to let go of power. These skills do not come easily—but they can be learned.

In teams that are largely self-directed, team members may choose to divvy up the leadership role so that each team member has part of it, or they may alternate as leader on a weekly, monthly, or quarterly basis.

- *Team members* are selected for their specific skills and strengths, although training may also build the skills the team needs. The role of team members is to do what they do best to achieve the goal. They pitch in where needed but focus on using their unique talents. Team members may take on a portion of the responsibilities related to safety, quality, production, statistical process control charting, customer service, team relations, and communication.

For example, one organization development team at a large company has a team leader who is also a facilitator, two facilitators with high-level computer skills, one associate facilitator who handles logistics, one communications planner and one support staff. This group can meet a variety of needs in the organization because of varied and complementary roles they play.

According to Kevin Androsian, former Human Resources Manager for Energy Distribution at DTE Energy, team members can also take on such roles as *timekeeper* and *scribe* to facilitate the work of the team and keep it on track. The timekeeper's job is to establish starting and ending times for meetings, and nudge the team back to the agenda when they stray off. The scribe's job is to keep a record of team proceedings and *lessons learned*. The scribe may want to develop a team notebook or database of lessons learned to which team members can refer when needed.

- The *facilitator* provides the process and tools for managing and documenting meetings effectively. The team leader, a specially trained member of the organization, or when appropriate, an outside facilitator, may fill the team facilitator role.

- *Resource people* join the team as needed. Their role is to support the team with information, expertise, or knowledge. They come and go, but share the team's goals while they work together.

Do the Keys Fit the Locks? (Matching Roles and Responsibilities)

Materials

- Copy of Vision and Goals (typed or on cards)
- Flip chart paper
- Large supply of 5″ × 8″ cards
- Markers
- Masking tape

Procedure

1. The team leader or facilitator posts the vision and goals generated in the previous exercise (on 5″ × 8″ cards or flip chart paper).
2. The team brainstorms the responsibilities necessary to achieve each goal. Team members write each responsibility on a 5″ × 8″ card and post these cards on the wall.
3. After about seven minutes of brainstorming, team members sort and match the responsibilities that go with each role.
4. The team may want to create duplicate cards for responsibilities, such as customer service, that are common to all roles.
5. One person from the team can transcribe the roles with related responsibilities and distribute a copy to each team member. He or she may alternatively take pictures with a digital camera and have a permanent record that way.

Time required

1–2 hours

Tips for Best Use

- Brainstorming on cards works especially well for this activity. Team members can easily sort the cards into groups or headings.
- Sticky notes are a good alternative to cards.
- The team may plan to revisit the roles and responsibilities list in later stages of team development when members are more skilled, or when cross-training has occurred.

Expected Results

Ownership of responsibilities is greater when the team generates the list together. Through discussion, team members better understand each others' roles, which improves teamwork and mutual support. Also, with the vision and goals displayed in front of the team, alignment within the team is more likely, while non-value-added work is less likely.

Caution Flag

Team members need to take care not to overload any given role. If a role has too many responsibilities, team members can break it down into two smaller roles. Team members may want to switch roles from time to time as well, so any one person will not become too associated with specific responsibilities.

Team Billboard (Making a Team Identity Poster)

Teams work best when they are task-oriented *and* relationship-oriented, when they have specific goals or milestones to achieve, and when they think of themselves as a team. The more quickly a team begins to think of itself as an entity, the more team members start working together toward a shared vision. One simple way to speed this process along is to have the team create a team "billboard" in the form of a chart or poster. The team must work together to create the billboard—and they can have a lot of fun in the process.

Materials

- A large piece of poster board
- Markers
- Magazines for cutting out appropriate pictures
- Scissors
- Glue sticks

Procedure

The team draws or otherwise creates a team billboard that can include some or all the following elements:

- Team Name (can be an acronym or other memorable designation, and can be as unusual as the team wishes)
- Team Logo (can be a diagram or a picture, and can use words and colors as well)
- Team Motto (a saying or slogan related to the team's purpose, values, composition, or preferred way of working)
- Team Goals (specific, measurable, challenging yet attainable, relevant, and timely)
- Team Members' Names and Roles (may include titles, actual or designated, and Communication Style from the CARStyles™ Inventory)
- Photographs of team members or possibly a group photograph
- Other items the team wants to add

Time Required

1–2 hours

Tips for Best Use

- This tool is most appropriate in the early part of the Orientation stage. However, if the team has not already made a billboard, they can benefit from doing so at any time.
- This creative activity encourages team members to have fun, which always strengthens team cohesion.
- The billboard hanging in the team's meeting room serves as a reminder of being part of a team.
- Team members may also want to consider selecting T-shirts or caps that display their team identity, much like the uniforms that racing teams wear.

Expected Results

Team members will have fun completing the team billboard. They will be free to use their imaginations and be as creative as they wish. They'll probably develop a team motto and logo, and these will add to their sense of belonging to the team. They will have a visual reminder of who they are—and seeing it will help remind them of their responsibilities to each other.

Real-Life Companies
Use Posters to Good Effect

An automotive supplier manufacturing plant implemented the Fast Start Teamwork™ process. Each intact work team, throughout all shifts, created their team billboard. The company prominently displayed the posters in the employee entrance and near work stations. A third shift team went one step further. The "Blue Crescents" chose their name because they worked the midnight shift. They baked and decorated crescent-shaped sugar cookies and distributed them to everyone throughout the plant. Everyone knew their quality improvements by their blue crescent signature on report sheets.

In another manufacturing facility, the shop floor plant rearranged work flow and processes into "focused factories." The three shifts in each focused factory agreed to an overall team identity. They hung their posters on the wall and then went a step further. They painted their work areas in the team colors and created a very colorful and clean plant environment with clearly defined work areas. The teams took so much pride in their new work area that a visitor walking through the area might hear these words, "Hey, watch it, we just mopped that floor!"

Ownership Matters

It is important that the team prepares the team billboard themselves. Otherwise, the chart may not serve its intended purpose of uniting the team. This result occurred in one company, when a department manager called for "team-building consultation." She was new to the company and eager to improve productivity, quality and customer service. Her department was the administrative support staff of a 30-person technical consulting firm.

At the first team meeting, the new manager displayed a lovely picture of the team as she saw it. In the picture, a train engine traveled through the countryside, on a track with a station in the background. Elaborate words explained that she was the engine, "pulling" the team forward. The coal car represented the members of the work group providing the power and energy for the team, while the passengers in the other cars were the rest of the organization they served. The countryside was the community where the office was located.

Elaborate as the poster was, it did not serve its purpose. Neither the staff nor anyone else in the firm provided input toward it. The poster remained on the wall in the manager's office collecting dust.

In contrast, the president of a 40-person company desired more teamwork between three distantly located offices. Employees came together for a two-day off-site and implemented Fast Start Teamwork™ activities along with a plan for future improvements. Their team billboard generated a lot of energy. The billboard was so dynamic that the president decided he would use it for the new corporate logo and image. What an exciting outcome for this newly energized team!

People find it much easier to work for the success of a corporate image they've helped create.

Strengthen
the Team's Identity

One important way to keep the team's identity strong is to communicate well, the way racing teams do.

In racing, several systems of communication exist: drivers

stay in constant touch with members of their racing team via two-way radios, and they post spotters in the stands to keep an eye on the track from a higher vantage point and report what they see. Yet the communication system that most people associate with auto racing is the flags. These colorful pieces of fabric waving in the breeze are a distinct part of the racetrack ambiance. The eight flags commonly used in racing, with colors and meanings, are listed below:

- GREEN—Indicates the start of a race or the restart after a caution period

- YELLOW—Indicates unsafe conditions on the track. Tells the driver to slow down, maintain current position, and not pass

- RED—Tells drivers to stop the race due to unsafe conditions

- BLUE WITH A YELLOW DIAGONAL STRIPE—Tells drivers to let faster cars or cars behind pass

- WHITE—Tells drivers that they are on the last lap of the race

- BLACK—Tells drivers to go immediately to the pits for consultation

- YELLOW WITH DOUBLE RED VERTICAL STRIPES— Indicates oil or debris on the track

- CHECKERED—Tells drivers, and everyone else, that the race has been won

Team members may not communicate with each other effectively. Personal agendas may suddenly emerge, or long-standing disagreements may escalate. Teams often avoid dealing with these types of situations that lead to conflict between team members. Poorly managed conflict like this can easily throw teams off the track.

Like the oil that makes an engine function smoothly, effective forms of communication such as racing flags help team members work together with less friction.

Visual and Verbal Team Symbols

Manufacturing organizations often use a visual system similar to the flags for communicating quickly or setting a tone. For example, a *kanban* card counting system uses cards of various colors to track production and materials needed for work-in-progress for many companies. Lights communicate the need for consultation with a team leader or maintenance support for others. Teams frequently display Statistical Process Control, Quality and Safety charts to communicate progress toward their goals. Suppliers, customers, and employees easily understand these visual messages.

Most communication symbols, particularly verbal ones, develop naturally, usually in the early phases of team development. Team members together often define the meaning of the communication symbol.

For example, a verbal expression that conveys a vivid visual image known primarily to the team can develop over time. "The geese are on the pond" is one such expression from a small assembly plant in Michigan. The phrase literally means that geese have landed in the air conditioning pond and trouble will result from clogging of the system. For teams in this company, the words provide a quick and colorful way to say, "We've got trouble." Another example is the phrase, "The alligators are circling." It serves the same function for some organizations as caution flags do for race drivers. The phrase communicates the idea that trouble is brewing.

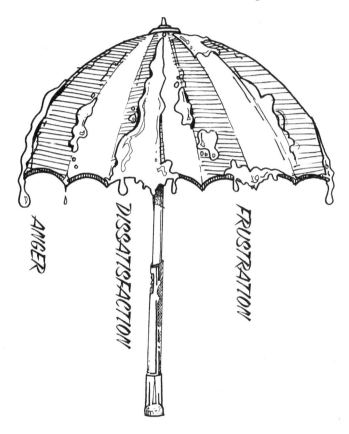

Someone draws an umbrella to remind a team member dealing with a difficult customer to let the unkind words and anger flow off the umbrella and away.

A Secretary of State office in Michigan uses a symbol of an umbrella that helps people to communicate with each other when a team member is dealing with a difficult customer. The office team attended a training seminar together where the presenter suggested the idea of raising an imaginary umbrella when faced with a disgruntled customer. The idea was that the unkind words and anger would flow off the umbrella and away from the employee. In this particular office, when a customer is berating a staff person, someone draws an umbrella on a scrap of paper and slides it over to the employee. This action breaks the tension, reminds the employee to stay calm, and communicates, "I'm here if you need me."

Ray Evernham describes how such verbal and visual symbols worked to his racing team's advantage when he tells how he and Jeff Gordon, the driver for whom he was formerly crew chief, communicated during a race. They didn't want to fall into patterns or tip off the competition about their next pitstop. Since everybody could hear them on the scanners, they learned to use code words to signal, for example, whether they were changing two tires or four. Sometimes, when the car was running well, Jeff would get on the radio and complain to Ray that the steering was tight, a code to indicate that he was about to pass another driver. And that driver's crew chief would say to his driver, "Yeah, Gordon can't pass you right now, because he's tight." The driver would leave a little opening and—boom—Gordon was past him.

Evernham describes team synergy when he says, "I surround [my guys] with ideas about teamwork. I read every leadership book I can get my hands on. One thing that I took from my reading is the idea of a *circle of strength*. When the Rainbow Warriors (Jeff Gordon's race team) met, we always put our chairs in a circle. That's a way of saying that we're stronger as a team than we are on our own."

A team at one of Michigan's electric utilities uses a candle as a team symbol. The pottery candleholder shows a team—four people with arms intertwined. During team meetings, team members light a votive that sits in the middle of the circle the four figures create. The candle flame reminds the members of this team that they are working together toward a shared vision.

Communication among team members occurs more readily when team members are in the "team frame of mind." Visual and tactile symbols such as the circle of strength or a candle, or verbal expressions with special meanings, unite a team and create a supportive and encouraging atmosphere. Teams may want to consider selecting their own symbol and using it as a routine part of team meetings.

Ground Rules or Core Values Set the Tone

Ground Rules are statements team members develop together to guide how they work together. Core Values or Guiding Principles are statements of how the team plans to work with their suppliers and serve customers. Sometimes these are different sets of statements. However, many times one set of statements serves both purposes.

In auto racing, the sponsor selects a driver based not so much on a conviction that he will win consistently, but rather on whether the driver shares the sponsor's values and marketing image. According to Ned Jarrett, "The sponsor thinks, 'Here is a driver that fits our image of our company.'"

The joint union-management team mentioned previously created the following set of core values:

- Tell the Truth
- Respect, Show Respect
- Be Fair, Treat Others Fair
- Recognize Jobs Well Done
- Keep Promises
- Take Pride in our Work
- Promote Continuous Learning

These simply worded, yet effective, core values spelled out how the team members would treat each other, their suppliers and their customers. Task teams helped define each statement, so there was a common understanding of each. They then used these statements as an assessment tool (similar to *Take a Team Test Drive*, page 116) to identify opportunities for improvement and to track improvement over time.

A training department in a plant setting created the following ground rules or *Rules for the Road*. These statements are congruent with this team's overall organizational values:

- Maintain team focus
- Be courteous, listen to each other
- Be open minded to the viewpoints of others
- Allow conflict of ideas, avoid conflict of personality style
- Be creative, challenge sacred cows

- Be customer driven
- Embrace diversity
- Be flexible
- Be optimistic and celebratory

Rules for the Road (Ground Rules/Core Values)

Materials

- Copies of Mission and Vision
- Flip chart paper
- 5" × 8" cards in various colors
- Markers
- Masking tape

Procedure

1. The team leader or facilitator posts the mission and vision on the wall.
2. The team brainstorms ideas for rules individually, using 5" × 8" cards.
3. They discuss, sort, and consolidate ideas by grouping the individual contributions into natural themes.
4. Together, they write the actual statements that will express these ideas.
5. Someone on the team prints and posts the *Rules for the Road* in the team meeting room.

Time Required

1–2 hours. May be completed over two meetings

Tips for Best Use

- The team needs to develop their own *Rules for the Road* so they will have ownership.
- Taking adequate time to ensure common understanding of the statements is helpful.
- The team needs to consider how they will measure these statements.

Expected Results

Some members of the team will test these statements right away. At first, it may feel as if the team has taken several backward steps. Team members need to address the behavior of the person who is violating an agreed-upon rule. Either the person will need to change his or her behavior, or the team will need to change or adjust the rule.

Testing will subside as the team moves from Organization to Data Flow. In general, having *Rules for the Road* to refer to will help the team resolve issues that surface.

Caution Flag

It's easy to create too many *Rules for the Road* and not to plan ahead how to implement them. These statements provide the opportunity for team members to use a feedback process to address getting off track from the core values. The team may want to discuss what it means to violate a ground rule and plan how to handle the person who does it. Otherwise the rules become meaningless. Successful teams hold each other accountable!

A Fast Start Teamwork™ Approach to Reducing Road Rage (Managing Conflict)

The beginning stages of building a team are often exciting and fun. But sooner or later, in the Storming stage, conflict will show its face, like a pothole waiting to throw a driver off balance. Different work and communication styles will clash. Disagreements and arguments may erupt, sometimes over team leadership, roles and responsibilities, or work assignments. For most teams, Storming is the most difficult stage to get through.

In fact, the best teams *thrive* on diversity of communication style, skills, and work preferences These differences broaden the team's perspective and add wisdom. But they also

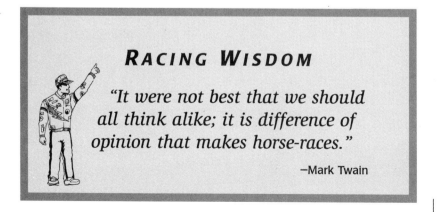

RACING WISDOM

"It were not best that we should all think alike; it is difference of opinion that makes horse-races."

—Mark Twain

make conflict between team members inevitable. When conflict shows up, a team leader, facilitator, or outside consultant has several options. He or she can:

- Encourage team members to set disagreements aside for the present and focus on task rather than on personality differences.

- Help the team look beyond their differences to the vision they share and focus on that. This may be a good time to consider one of the variations of *Tuning In to the Same Frequency,* a vision-sharing activity (see page 62).

- Suggest that team members do the *Go as Far as You Can* activity (see pages 127 and 214). Team members will understand the way in which conflict can actually produce poorer results for the company as a whole.

- Introduce a feedback tool such as *Four Quarters Feedback.* This tool provides a structured feedback process that often helps team members understand each other better and prevents them from basing their behavior on false assumptions.

- Lead the team in discussing the conflict from the perspective of ideas rather than the perspective of personalities.

- Encourage and reward flexibility in communication style. The racing story following demonstrates how this kind of flexibility works.

Flexibility in Communication Style Leads to Success

Flexibility in communication style is a real benefit during times of stress and conflict. People who can adjust their style when needed are valuable people and may contribute in a big way to team success. For example, when Ned Jarrett talks about the personalities and roles of his son, Dale, and Dale's crew chief, Todd Parrott, he points out how they sometimes change roles when it benefits the team effort to do so.

"I listen to Dale and Todd on the headset," he says, "when I'm not working a broadcast. Todd is normally a competitor and can be easily riled. Dale is usually calm by nature. Yet Dale will get upset when the car is not running exactly right, and Todd will say, kind of soothingly, 'Okay, we'll get it fixed.'

"At Rockingham a few weeks ago, I heard Todd say, 'Be smooth, let that thing roll into the turn. Don't use too much brake.' That has a much more calming effect that saying something like, 'Son of a gun, you're not driving that car right! You're driving too deep!' Dale and Todd have different personalities, and they use that well."

This story shows how Todd Parrott, a typically more expressive person, was able to change his style in order to calm his teammate. Their experience with each other indicated the need for flexibility. Todd adjusted so that Dale could be cool-headed, because the team needed him to be cool-headed at that point.

Four Quarters Feedback

Four Quarters Feedback helps people state clearly what they would like the person on the other side of the conflict to do, as well as to understand that person's perspective. In a conflict, people often make assumptions about another's behavior and judge it accordingly, thus deepening the conflict and shutting down communication. Using *Four Quarters Feedback* allows team members to express their feelings and check out the assumptions they've made at the same time. It also gives the person on the other side of the disagreement a chance to explain if the person hasn't interpreted accurately.

Procedure

1. The people in a conflict or other situation that requires feedback take turns giving each other feedback according to the model in the figure below:

FIGURE 11: Four Quarters Feedback*

When you say . . . (say actual data)

I feel . . . (happy/sad/angry/afraid)

And I think/judge/assume/wonder . . .

I'd like . . . (specific actions from the other person)

Then inquire:
What's your view?

---

* From "Leading Learning Communities" by Fred Kaufman, 1996

2. To follow the model, each person may do the following things:

- Talk first about the actual data of the conflict, the observable behavior involved. Be careful not to incorporate your assessments of the behavior into the conversation, but to limit your comments to the behavior itself.

- Next talk about your feelings in response to the data you've just described. Restrict this to feelings only—happy, sad, angry, afraid, or whatever the feeling.

- Next describe the attributions you have made as a result of the data and your feelings. Be sure to own each attribution as your own, and not talk about it as if it is the "truth."

- Describe what you'd like the other person to do in the future. Be specific and concrete, and talk about actions that fall into the realm of observable data.

- Then inquire: "What's your view?" and invite the other person to give you feedback in the same manner.

Time Required

15 minutes for both people to express their views
Up to 15 extra minutes for debriefing

Tips for Best Use

- Team members will want to learn to use *Four Quarters Feedback* early in the team-building process.

- Team members will want to practice using the model rather than waiting until conflict erupts and emotions are running high.

- After team members have given feedback to each other, they can debrief with the team leader or facilitator.

  —Do they have a clearer understanding of the other person's actions than before?

  —Are they satisfied with the results that using the model has helped them achieve?

  —Will each person be able to do as the other has asked?

  —If not, what are some alternative solutions that might work for both parties?

Suppose that one person in a team continually interrupts another. Finally the one who is being interrupted decides to give feedback about this situation. The two people using *Four Quarters Feedback* might sound as follows:

> **PERSON 1** *Pat, I'd like to talk to you about something that bothers me a lot. When you interrupt me while I'm talking, I feel irritated and angry. I assume that you're not interested in what I'm saying and not really listening to me. I'd like you to wait until I finish speaking before you say what you need to say. What's your view?*

> **PERSON 2** *I didn't really realize I was interrupting you. Can you draw my attention to it at the moment I do it next? Once I'm aware, I'll be more able to stop.*

Expected Results

Team members will learn that they do make assumptions about another's behavior that may not be valid. They will learn to separate observable data from the feeling they have about that data. They will learn over time and with practice to express their feelings without attaching assessments and attributions. They will learn to ask specifically for what they want from another person. Finally, they will learn to give and accept feedback without reacting instinctively in a negative way.

Caution Flag

It's a challenge for some people to limit their comments to observable data. The team leader or facilitator may want to work with people to help them develop skill in giving and receiving feedback. Otherwise, techniques like this one quickly lose their value.

Diagnosing the Type of Conflict or Difference

Materials

- Flip chart paper
- Markers

Procedure

1. The team leader or facilitator draws a continuum similar to the following figure on the flip chart paper

FIGURE 12: Chart of Differences

> *Differences*
>
> 1. FACT: something one knows to be true   EASY
>   Ex: anything you can count, look up, measure
>
> 2. GOAL: the "what" we are to achieve
>   Ex: 100% customer satisfaction
>
> 3. METHOD: "how" we will achieve it
>   Ex: improve quality, lower prices, improve delivery
>
> 4. VALUE: basic beliefs we all hold
>   Ex: "the customer is always right"   DIFFICULT

2. The team leader or facilitator says: "All conflict can be defined as one of these differences. Which category or categories does this conflict fit?"
3. The team discusses each category in relation to the problem.
4. Conflicts along the continuum are progressively more difficult to manage. In fact, the team will probably not be able to resolve differences in the "values" category and will need to learn to manage the conflict these differences cause instead—or even to harness the energy in them in support of the team's vision by agreeing to honor all values rather than fight over them or look diligently for the common ground the polarized positions may share.

Time Required

15–60 minutes depending on the type of difference, the temperament of the people, and the severity of the conflict.

Tips for Best Use

- The team leader or facilitator should be willing to discuss differences at any time conflict threatens to destroy team synergy. The leader needs to be comfortable with the *uncomfortableness* of appropriate conflict.

- Appropriate conflict is defined as the conflict of ideas, not of personalities. Any conflict resulting from challenging ideas, outcomes, results, or goals is appropriate, because it challenges assumptions and sacred cows.

- If the difference is not within the ability of the team to change, they may discuss how to use it creatively and learn from it. Sometimes team members can negotiate behavior that will bridge the differences between them.

- If the difference is a communication style, reviewing how each style helps or hinders team success can help team members to appreciate their differences.

Expected Results

Since conflict is inevitable, this is a good time for the team to talk about and understand how the term conflict *management* (make it work for us) is different from conflict *resolution* (make it go away). Managing the conflict can actually result in a higher quality outcome. In fact, sometimes just the act of categorizing the conflict and collecting new data can move the team forward.

Caution Flag

The team may get bogged down in the conflict issue. They may become so upset, they stall. If they stall, they may begin to withdraw from discussion or fail to meet with each other. At this point, successful teams focus on the vision or goal rather than on interpersonal issues and get going again.

A Real-Life Conflict Management Story

In a large company, the leader of a team was involved in numerous meetings and was often absent from the office. One of her team members felt it was impossible to have any coherent communication with her team leader because of her busy schedule. Bad feelings were growing between the two. The team leader called in an outside consultant to facilitate a face-to-face conversation and negotiate a solution. Both people involved were able to take a fresh look at some misunderstandings that had occurred between them. The team leader's meeting schedule was impossible to change, but she agreed to have a phone conversation with the team member at a regular time each week. Both parties were satisfied with this arrangement, and their ability to work together has improved steadily with the consistent weekly contact.

laps to go!

Data Flow—
Handling the Curves

"This team should be able to focus on the primary goal, which is to go out and compete on Sunday afternoons.

—Brett Bodine, NASCAR driver

FIGURE 13: A Guide to Chapter 6—Data Flow

Steps Along the Pathway to the Checkered Flag	Fast Start Teamwork™ Tools	Location in this Chapter
Assess the team's potential	Take a Team Test Drive	Page 116
Learn about each others' strengths, talents, skills and preferences	High Octane Teams

The Loyal Fan | Page 120

Page 122 |
Appreciate the value of teamwork	The Auto Parts Store Challenge	Page 125
Reduce competition between team members or between teams	Go as Far As You Can	Page 127
Add talent to the team if needed	CARStyles™ Inventory, revisited	Page 67 Chapter 4
Scan the environment	News from the Racetrack and the World	Page 132

Measurement Is an Important Part of Data Flow

Research increasingly shows that the way to high performance is to build strength rather than "fix" weakness. (Buckingham and Coffman, 1999) Consequently, team members must understand their strengths and focus on these. They also need to be sure to add any talent the team needs. In these ways, they build the team's capacity to take the checkered flag.

Teams may want to assess their current situation and identify their team potential in order to give themselves a benchmark. The team can conduct an assessment very easily and quickly by taking a team "test drive."

Take a Team Test Drive

Materials

A copy of the *Take a Team Test Drive* worksheet for each team member (see page 209).

Procedure

1. Each team member completes the assessment questionnaire individually, taking 5–10 minutes to do so.
2. The team leader or facilitator tallies the team members' responses and calculates the mean (average) and the range (low and high scores) for each question.

3. The team debriefs each other on the responses, talking about what needs to happen for their scores on the various items to improve.

4. The team can use this questionnaire again later in the team-building process. They can compare their results at that time to the present results, and measure their progress as a team.

Time Required

5–10 minutes for the questionnaire
Up to an hour to debrief the team

Tips for Best Use

- Team members fill out the questionnaire without any help from anyone or conversation with anyone.

- The team can do another activity while the team leader or facilitator tallies up the scores and gets the team averages—or they can complete the question-naire at one team meeting and debrief at the next.

- The results of this assessment can give teams a good basis for choosing tools that will improve their ability to develop synergy and take the checkered flag.

Expected Results

Each team member has a chance to express an opinion and con-tribute to a group result. Team members will learn indirectly about the qualities of a good team. They will automatically create a picture in their minds about their preferred team future as they consider the different team qualities. Team members may be surprised at their scores and develop a strong wish to improve them.

The joint union-management team mentioned previously used an alternative to the *Take a Team Test Drive* assessment. They used their core values as the basis for an assessment. Internal facilitators distributed the short assessment throughout the workforce, tallied the means (averages) and provided feedback to the plant. The steering committee identified three opportunities for improvement based on scores. Six months later, the facilitators redistributed the assessment, compared the results to the first assessment, and reported the results of the comparisons. Teams may want to create their own benchmark assessment using their own standards in a similar way.

Caution Flag

Some team members may not like the idea of assessment. It's easy to place too much emphasis on improving numbers. This assessment is not in any way intended for holding *individuals* accountable for making the numbers go up. The purpose is rather to identify areas in which the *team* can improve.

Focusing on Team Strength

A great tool to help move the team forward is the *High Octane Teams* profile. Especially in the times of conflict and stress, focusing on strengths is a positive thing to do. Racing team members often mention how another person on the team helps the team stay focused, or interfaces well with sponsors and media, or "knows when to be quiet," as one driver said about his spotter.

George Winchester and Russ Yeager, two businessmen in Jackson, Michigan, are teammates who build on their respective strengths in their workplace. George is a plant manager with 24 years of manufacturing experience. He sees his strength as "making business and people successful." Russ is a human resources manager with 13 years of business experience. He describes himself as "a teacher and implementer of change."

George and Russ have teamed up twice in two different plants for two different companies to bring about strategic changes that have improved the bottom line. Together, they are a *special team*. George tends to be the *Full Size Sedan*, rolling over anyone who resists change. Russ, the more congenial *Minivan*, mends fences. George describes it this way:

"I am more 'shoot from the hip,' and I don't always realize people don't understand until the next day. I go to Russ to discuss the situation, but usually people have already come to him for explanation, and now they understand. I don't intend to be aggressive, but it comes out that way. I tend to put people on the spot. Russ is good at letting people come to him and ask for help."

George and Russ are different in age, personality, and skill sets, but they share a similar value system. This, they agree, is what makes the difference. These two men have meshed their very different styles into synergy, which tends to speed checkered flag results.

High Octane Teams

Materials

- Copy of *High Octane Teams* worksheet for each person on the team (see page 212)
- Flip chart
- Markers

Procedure

1. The team leader or facilitator hands out the one-page questionnaire in advance of a team meeting and asks people to prepare their responses.
2. Each person on the team completes the form.
3. Each person shares this information with other team members at the team meeting.
4. The team leader or facilitator records the strengths and skills on a flip chart under the appropriate headings:
   a. Technical Skills of the Team
   b. Interpersonal Strengths
5. He or she *does not* place names beside each strength and skill. The goal is to paint a picture of the team's collective strengths and skills. This "big picture" serves to show the high level of skill the team has, which will increase the team's confidence. At subsequent meetings, the team can brainstorm missing strengths and skills and identify additional members or resource people they will invite to participate.

6. Team members share hidden/unused talents and preferences for work assignments next. The purpose is to improve understanding and respect for each other. At subsequent meetings, the group may use this information to redistribute work assignments and identify additional or different responsibilities.

Time Required

One to two hours, depending on the size of the team and level of preparation

Tips for Best Use

- In the meeting, it's best not to rush this process.
- When completed, someone on the team can type up the information on the flip charts and distribute a copy to team members.
- Information from this activity may become part of the agenda for subsequent team meetings.

Expected Results

Team members may be surprised at the variety of skills the team has—how "high octane" the team really is. They will understand each other better and respect each other more. They will gain confidence in the ability of the team to be successful. They will have an opportunity to improve team functioning by identifying missing strengths or skills. They will also have the opportunity to redistribute work assignments and responsibilities in a more efficient and effective manner.

Teams Can Assign Roles Based on Preferences

A training department team used this activity successfully to reorganize their work process. Previously, team members served as "account reps" for a particular functional area in the organization. That meant each person met with the internal client, assessed needs, designed training (or negotiated with a vendor), presented the training, and evaluated the results. This "whole job" process wasn't satisfying to the team members, and it put people in conflict over limited resources.

The *High Octane Teams* activity identified each team member's strengths and preferences. The team then reorganized into "skill units." Analytical *Utility Vehicle* types teamed with congenial *Minivan* types to meet with the client and assess needs. Out-in-front *Sporty Coupes* presented the training, while *Full Size Sedans* evaluated the results and interfaced with management for the necessary resources to meet the needs of the department team.

Customer satisfaction surveys and training evaluation assessments of Key Result Areas showed the training department team achieved checkered flag results consistently.

The Loyal Fan

Materials

This is a variation of the *High Octane Teams* tool and requires the same materials:

- Copy of *High Octane Teams* worksheet for each person on the team (see page 212)
- Flip chart
- Markers

Procedure

1. Using the same worksheet as in *High Octane Teams,* team members pair up, interview each other, and record the partner's responses on a blank form.
2. Then each in turn introduces the other by strengths, skills and preferences just the way a loyal race fan might describe a favorite driver.
3. The facilitator or team leader encourages each person to really "sell" the other person and have fun with the process.
4. The facilitator places strengths and talents on flip chart paper as before, under the appropriate headings:
   a. Technical Skills of the Team
   b. Interpersonal Strengths
5. Again, the team leader or facilitator does not identify strengths by individual names. Rather, he or she builds a picture of team strengths and skills.

Time Required

One to two hours

Tips for Best Use

- The team leader or facilitator needs to be vigilant about equal time for "selling."

- The facilitator or team leader may want to encourage more energy from the quiet and reserved *Utility Vehicle* individuals.

Expected Results

This alternate activity tends to generate a lot of enthusiasm and energy within the group. People often enjoy their time of being in the spotlight.

Appreciating the Value of Teamwork

When a team is in turmoil, they tend to think that being part of a team is useless. "I can do better by myself," a disgruntled team member might think. This is a good time to share team success stories such as the one below and to use the tool that follows to help team members appreciate the value of teamwork.

A Teamwork Success Story

The ingredients of a great restaurant include great food and atmosphere. *Radius*, a restaurant in Boston's financial district, has added another ingredient: "a heaping scoop of teamwork." The teamwork starts in the kitchen, which is divided into stations—such as the meat station or the pastry station. Two people team up at each station, and they have full responsibility for their part of the meal. The restaurant staff is also involved in a series of meetings that reinforce both the spirit and practice of teamwork. One weekly meeting focuses on front-line service. Another daily meeting focuses on behind-the-scenes operations. A third daily service meeting includes all of the wait staff, the floor managers, and the hosts and hostesses. This meeting focuses on the customers—who's got reservations, who's been to the restaurant before, what they do. *Radius* has gained a loyal following as a result of teamwork—and a growing reputation in the industry. It's on its way to achieving its vision of being ranked among the top 25 restaurants in the country. In sum, it's achieving checkered flag results.

The Auto Parts Store Challenge

Materials

A copy of the *Auto Parts Store Challenge* for each person (see page 213)

Procedure

1. Working independently, each person reads the case and then computes the mathematical solution.
2. Working as a team, they discuss the solution and come to an agreement on the one correct solution.

3. The team leader or facilitator allows the team to struggle with agreeing to the solution. The various communication styles will emerge, and each will suggest a different method of understanding the problem and agreeing to the solution.

4. If the team offers an incorrect solution, the team leader or facilitator challenges them to try again.

5. When the team offers the correct solution, the team leader or facilitator debriefs them on the process of arriving at the correct solution.

Time Required

30 minutes

Tips for Best Use

- The team will benefit more from this activity if the team leader or facilitator states that this is a "mathematical problem with only one correct answer."

- The team leader or facilitator takes note of people's communication behavior and ties this back to CARStyles ™ during the debrief.

- The team can use this activity at any time in the teamwork process. Good times to consider it are when the team members are learning about each other's work styles, when the team is struggling with an issue and needs a little break, or when the team needs a warm-up activity to prepare for more difficult work.

Expected Results

The primary purpose of this activity is help team members appreciate the value of having teammates with different styles. During the activity, people will see each other's work style in action and learn more about the style and each other. Recalling the fun they had solving this problem may ease a rough team moment when they're working together in the future.

Caution Flag

None

Go As Far As You Can

This activity can often help tremendously to reduce tendencies toward inappropriate competition among or between teams. It shows how much more profitable teamwork can be than working alone or worse yet, unknowingly working against each other. The exercise will show team members in a rather startling way how profound the acronym "**T**ogether **E**veryone **A**chieves **M**ore" really is.

Materials

Go As Far As You Can worksheets (see page 214)

Procedure

Follow the instructions as provided by the activity worksheet. This worksheet provides detailed suggestions for facilitating the activity.

Time Required

30 minutes to play the game
Up to one hour to debrief

Tips for Best Use

- The team leader or facilitator needs to be thoroughly familiar with the instrument before using it. He or she must feel comfortable handling the disruption that may occur.
- People need sufficient time to debrief thoroughly.
- Keep in mind that often team members become so engaged in the activity that feelings get hurt.
- Team members can tie this activity back to the CARStyles™ Inventory and discuss how their reactions helped or hindered the team.

Expected Results

Teams become actively engaged in the activity and they generally exhibit their personality styles in an obvious way. The debrief provides the opportunity to learn what happens when people don't focus on the overall team vision and goals, but instead work toward achieving their own personal agendas.

Caution Flag

This activity only works well in the early stages of team development. Typically a team that has already moved to Norming will realize the nature of the team goal and no competition or conflict will result.

CARStyles™ Show Up in Behavior

CARStyles™ behaviors that frequently emerge in the above activity include the following:

- The *Full Size Sedan* may become a tank and try to run over everyone else.
- The *Utility Vehicle* avoids conflict at all costs and will likely withdraw into an analytical abyss.
- The *Minivan* also prefers to avoid conflict, but likely will try to smooth things over.
- The outgoing *Sporty Coupe* may show off by throwing a temper tantrum that gets a lot of attention, but rarely solves anything.

In the discussion that results from this activity, people sometimes define the team, the goal, and their own role in unusual ways. This can happen in auto racing, too.

Add Talent to the Team

This is a good time to add talent to the team, if needed. An example from the field shows how the CARStyles™ Inventory or a similar instrument can be helpful. Aeroquip Corporation launched a green field plant (a plant just starting up with new construction) in New Haven, Indiana. The management team was getting organized. The team agreed to design the plant processes and workforce as a "self-directed" operation. The team used a four-component personality type model and the *High Octane Teams* profile to identify skills and strengths. They determined that the team was missing analytical skills. The plant manager was an expressive-driver with a good track record for getting results. The team needed to fill the quality manager position. The highly qualified person hired to fill the position was an analytical *Utility Vehicle* type. The plant manager did not instantly like the candidate, but he understood that his opposite was the best person to complete his team. Therefore, he trusted the team's decision to hire the person they determined was the best fit.

Industry Week magazine named this plant one of "America's Best Plants" in terms of productivity, quality and customer satisfaction. Paying attention to the earlier team-building process made the difference.

George Winchester and Russ Yeager also were successful in using a four-quadrant type of communication style profile and team strength profile to complete their team. Russ described the process. "We realized we had a void in the detail-oriented, get-it-done type person. We needed someone to keep us from glossing over all the things that were detail-oriented." They hired a new employee to fill those needs and who "still had the same values as us."

Any team can experience this difference. If, like the Aeroquip team and George and Russ, they've used Fast Start Teamwork™ tools and applied the GRIP model, they're up and running now. Team members are learning to understand and work with each

RACING WISDOM

"Drafting," a common race oc-currence based on physics, is an interesting example of un-usual teaming. Two cars racing to-gether, bumper-to-bumper, are faster than either car racing alone. This is speedway synergy, and it was dramatized by Tom Cruise and Nicole Kidman with two packets of artificial sweetener in the movie Days of Thunder.

At times, two competing race drivers will team up temporarily to pass another car. After they make the pass, they will suddenly separate and race each other again. For a split second, though, they shared one goal of passing the third car.

other. People have agreed to support the vision and goals, work within their roles and responsibilities, and support personality differences of other team members. Now it's time for the team to really make some progress toward the finish line.

Now team members need to scan their environment to make sure they're aware of what's happening around them that could affect their work. A simple way to do this is to agree to gather *News from the "Racetrack" and the World.*

News from the Racetrack and the World

Each person on the team agrees to keep an eye on anything related to the workings of the team. Based on their strengths and CARStyle™:

- People who like to read watch the newspapers
- People who like to surf the Internet do so
- People who are TV watchers pay attention to the news and commentary
- People who like to network spend more time than usual talking with people

Team members are looking for anything that could adversely or positively affect the team's vision and goals. New resources the team might use or news from the competition are examples. At regular meetings, they report their findings to the rest of the team. The team considers the new information and agrees to take appropriate action if required.

Gathering news from their organization and the world is an ongoing process teams engage in. Teams who become skilled at scanning the team's environment are more likely to achieve checkered flag results.

laps to go!

Taking the
Checkered Flag

Solving Problems—
Moving Toward the
Checkered Flag

"Failure is an opportunity to begin again, more intelligently."

—Henry Ford

FIGURE 14: A Guide for Chapter 7—Solving Problems

Steps Along the Pathway to the Checkered Flag	Fast Start Teamwork™ Tools	Location in this Chapter
Learn problem-solving skills and use them	FAST™ Problem Solving	Page 138
Learn how to build consensus	We're In This Car Together	Page 149
Clear obstacles to success	What's Driving This Car?	Page 153
Understand the team's scope	Control/No Control	Page 157
Measure Team Cohesion	Take a Team Test Drive, *Revisited*	Page 158
Refocus on the vision if needed	How Many Laps to Go?	Page 162
Adjust the strategy	Two Tires or Four?	Page 164
Celebrate!	Let the Driver Decide	Page 167

FAST Problem Solving

Fast Problem Solving is a spin-off of Dr. Greg Huszczo's 4-A Problem Solving Model.* (See *Tools for Team Excellence*, 1996).

The acronym FAST stands for **F**elt Need, **A**nalysis, **S**trategic Actions, and **T**esting. This model works equally well for solving problems or developing opportunities for improvement.

What Can Happen Without a Structured Problem-Solving Process

A woman once had a row of beautiful trees planted along the driveway that led to her house, planted there by the original owner.

Soon, she noticed that one of the trees didn't look so great and appeared to be suffering from some unknown problem. Its symptoms were poor growth, poor color, and an infestation of spider mites. She called the tree service.

The tree service suggested various solutions and tested them:

1. Put a drip hose on the tree for a few weeks because it was too dry. (The drip didn't help.)

---

* While earning her degree at Eastern Michigan University, Renée Merchant was part of a management class that used Huszczo's original 4-A Problem-Solving Model at an actual workplace as part of the curriculum. After graduating, she worked on the model and developed it further, as did Huszczo.

2. Use a chemical spray to kill the spider mites. (The spray killed the bugs, but it didn't help the tree.)
3. Use deep root fertilization to compensate for sandy soil. (Extra nutrients didn't help, though a year passed and the woman spent a lot of money.)
4. Repeat all of the above and add chemical injection into the tree's trunk. (Nor did the chemicals do the job.)

Finally, during year three, the tree died. When the people from the tree service removed the tree, there, covered by dirt, was the remnant of the root ball—and a tightly tied orange plastic cord that had held the root ball together. The cord had strangled the tree. The landscaper was a man accustomed to burlap-covered root balls tied with hemp. Not realizing that

This tree might not have died if the root cause of
its problem had been determined.

the orange plastic cord was not biodegradable, he had failed to cut it away.

The tree service suggested solutions without digging to the root cause of the problem. If they had been able *to discover the root cause* of this tree's problem, they'd have been able to save the tree. Instead, they were treating only the symptoms.

Teams must explore deeply enough to find the root cause of any Felt Need if they hope to be successful in solving a problem. Otherwise, like the tree doctors, they'll only treat symptoms and fail to work toward a "cure."

FAST™ Problem Solving

Materials

- Copies of the *FAST Problem-Solving Model*
- Evidence of the felt need of a problem or an opportunity for improvement
- Flip chart paper
- Markers

Procedure

Felt Need

1. The team leader or facilitator explains the model and how to use it.
2. The team documents the evidence of the Felt Need and establishes measures that will indicate success. "What's going

The FAST™ Problem-Solving Model

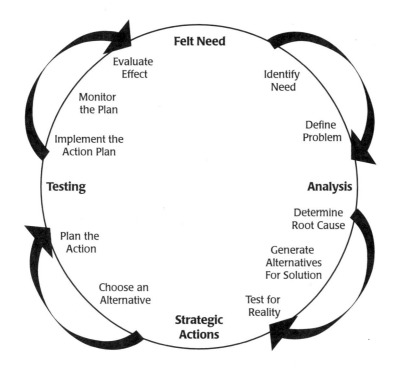

Felt Need

Evaluate Effect

Identify Need

Monitor the Plan

Define Problem

Implement the Action Plan

Testing

Analysis

Plan the Action

Determine Root Cause

Generate Alternatives For Solution

Choose an Alternative

Test for Reality

Strategic Actions

This process helps team members get to the root cause of a problem or think through an opportunity for improvement.

on here?" is a good question to ask. "What symptoms do we see?" is another.

Analysis

3. The team analyzes the problem by gathering data, including Statistical Process Control and benchmarking data if appropriate. They can draw process maps if that will help. They need to ask "Why?" over and over again until everyone agrees that they've found the root cause of the problem.

Strategic Actions

4. The team now brainstorms possible creative solutions to the problem. The group does not judge the solutions at this point. Rather, they encourage people to think creatively and make it safe for them to say whatever pops into their minds. The team needs to look at the problem from several different perspectives and call in resource people if necessary. Resource people could include front-line people.

5. The team develops a list of key criteria, i.e., quality, cost, customer satisfaction. Then the team tests each alternative against each criterion.

6. By consensus, the team chooses what appears to be the best solution, tests it on paper, and implements it.

7. The team plans the actions they will take, ensuring that the solution they select is acceptable to the people who must live with it. It's best to involve these people in the decision if possible, and at the very least, keep them informed. Then the team must:

   a. Determine who on the team will do what, where, when, and how.

   b. Plan for possible spin-off effects, both positive and negative.

   c. Keep an action plan record in order to hold people accountable.

Testing

8. Implement the plan—Just do it!

9. Monitor the plan.

10. Evaluate the plan—Did the solution achieve the goal and solve the problem?

a. If the answer is no, go back to Step 2. Redefine the problem, asking, "Did we arrive at the root cause or causes?

b. If the team has adequately defined the problem, go to Step 6—Choose an Alternative. Ask, "Can we modify our original solution to make it work?" "Would an alternative we rejected be a good choice now? Or, "Is there a new alternative we didn't think of before?"

Time Required

Varies according to the nature of the problem. Can be a short time, or a period of weeks or even months.

Tips for Best Use

- The team needs to be very thorough in gathering data to support the solution.

- Keeping careful records will help the team understand the process they used if they need to review it at a later date.

- Looking at the problem from various perspectives sometimes leads to highly creative solutions.

- It is helpful to visually display the FAST process as the team works on the solution. This encourages others in the organization to offer ideas and suggestions. Also, if another team is working on another aspect of the same problem, the visual display informs both teams if they are duplicating their work and provides the opportunity for the two teams to work together.

The following is a charting technique used at the Aeroquip New Haven, Indiana plant mentioned previously. Teams can easily copy the format onto flip chart paper and display the chart in the employee cafeteria or near the employee entrance.

FIGURE 15: Display Chart showing FAST™

Felt Need	Analysis
1. The felt need (starting point)	3. Root cause; ask "why"
2. Problem based on data	4. Alternatives
	5. Criteria for testing
Strategic Actions	**Testing**
6. Alternative selected	8. Implementation
7. Action Plan Who: What: Where: By when: How: (steps)	9. Monitor the plan 10. Evaluate: did it work?

Posting a chart like this one in a highly visible place encourages others to offer ideas to a team.

Expected Results

If the team adheres to all steps of the model, they will most likely solve the problem. They will feel a great sense of accomplishment. Whatever symptoms the problem was causing will diminish or go away—for example, costs will go down, productivity will go up, or quality will improve.

While all problem-solving models are simply analysis (taking the problem apart) and synthesis (putting the solution together), the Fast Problem Solving method is easy to remember and simple to implement. This model makes good use of the four communication styles. The *Utility Vehicle* will help collect data, the *Sporty Coupe* will be great at brainstorming, the *Minivan* will find resource people to help out, and the *Full Size Sedan* will keep the goal in mind and push toward a quick solution. And, of course, all the car types will want to go FAST.

Caution Flag

The team needs to be wary of "jumping to solutions" before determining the root cause of the problem. People, particularly *Full Size Sedans* and *Sporty Coupes,* may be reluctant to explore the problem in enough depth. The solution they choose that seems so obvious to them ("It's just common sense," they might say) may turn out to be just a quick fix, and the problem will almost certainly re-emerge later.

Three Real-Life Problem-Solving Stories

Success in a Manufacturing Plant

A supplier of automotive plastic parts was having an intermittent problem with quality of parts produced. A lack in consistency of the product produced resulted in quality and delivery problems. The supplier was rejecting and scrapping poor quality parts, and consequently making late deliveries to customers.

Felt Need

Intermittent quality problem, resulting from the fact that the parts produced were not always to specification. This problem was threatening the ability of the business to survive.

Analysis

Root cause analysis: asking "Why?"

- 1st "Why?"—Why are the parts bad?
- 1st response—The parts are bad because the resin delivered from the silo is bad.
- 2nd "Why?"—Why is the resin delivered from the silo bad?
- 2nd response—The resin delivered from the silo is bad because the delivery system is "dirty."
- Testing 2nd response—After analysis, we can say that the delivery system is "clean."
- 3rd "Why?"—So why is the resin bad?
- 3rd, and in this case root cause response—The resin is bad because the supplier is shipping out-of-spec resin.

Strategic Actions

Meet with the supplier and impose the same quality standards as those required by the plant's customers.

Testing

The team tracked every delivery of resin for quality and continued to track product. Quality improved, product delivery was on time, and the customer was satisfied. The plant kept an important business client.

Final Thought

Management empowered the hourly plant workers to meet with the supplier in question and work out the details. This was a real success story for this plant, because they began to implement the "tiered process"* common in the automotive industry. Their experience in this instance helped them to be more understanding of their customers' problems.

Successful Problem Solving in the Racing World

Teamwork and collaboration solved the problem of racecars becoming airborne during a spin. Working as a team, Gary Nelson, series director for NASCAR, Roush Industries, and Embry-Riddle Aeronautical University in Daytona, Florida, developed roof flaps. These *aerodynamic stabilizers*, as defined on the U.S. patent bearing Gary's name, are a significant safety feature. The flaps are mounted within the roofline of all NASCAR series vehicles. If a race car spins backwards or sideways, the flaps pop up and keep the car on the ground.

*See page 56.

While this team did not specifically use FAST™ Problem Solving, they did use the same principles: They felt a need; they analyzed the problem; they tried several solutions until they found the right one; and they tested it for success.

Staff at Eastern Michigan University Make a Difference

For several years, *Barriers to Learning* teams at Eastern Michigan University have worked to eliminate or remove process problems that were causing students and staff unnecessary difficulty. One such team had a spectacularly successful result because they used a problem-solving process.

Felt Need

A computer processing program used to process student refunds typically took more than 50 hours each week to run. This lengthy running time tied up the computer system which often failed to complete its work over the weekend.

Analysis

A team drew a process map and looked carefully at each segment of it. They thought of several possible solutions.

Strategic Actions

The team began a structured, documented process of testing each of the possible solutions. Some of the suggested solutions failed to make any significant difference. But one made a huge difference. The team discovered that the program had been processing students who were no longer at Eastern as well as those who were currently registered. They reprogrammed it to process only current students.

Testing

The new programming enabled the team to cut the processing time by nearly *two-thirds*, from more than 50 hours *to less than 12*. This dramatic reduction in time use opened a bottleneck that had caused this university community serious difficulty.

Getting People Involved

Good team leaders everywhere want to get team members involved in the problem-solving process. For example, Eric Brevig, visual-effects supervisor for *Industrial Light and Magic*, a group that provides visual effects for films, says, "Even when I have an idea or a plan, I try to invite people to be part of the problem solving. That way, they feel like part of the team—and they usually come up with a better idea than mine."

Not only will the ideas be better, but the team will be more willing to implement them since they've helped create them.

Building Consensus

Most effective teams decide early in their team-building process to make decisions by consensus. Consensus embodies the advantages a team approach brings. It includes the perspectives and knowledge of the various team members and motivates them to make the solution work.

Doing *We're In This Car Together* will help team members understand the meaning of consensus, and practice building it as well. In building consensus, the process involves building a big agreement by constructing little agreements.

This process can help teams identify their goals and objectives, agree to core values, plan projects, and remove non-value-added work. It has many other applications as well.

WISDOM FROM ANOTHER RACING SPORT

The team of adventure racers described earlier has a firm policy: They make every decision by consensus. "If that means that the whole team stops to spend an hour debating which way to head through a canyon, so be it," says a team member. "Over the course of six or seven days of nonstop competition, you can't look to the same person for everything."

We're In This Car Together (Building Consensus)

Materials

- 5″ × 8″ cards
- Flip chart paper
- Markers

Procedure

1. The team leader or facilitator defines consensus for the team: It's not necessarily total agreement, and it's not a majority vote. Dannemiller Tyson Associates define it in their book *Whole-Scale™ Change: Unleashing the Magic in Organizations* as "70% committed and 100% willing to support." If even one person says, "I cannot support that decision," there is no consensus. Team members *can* express doubts or concerns, but they must agree to support the final decision.
2. The team leader or facilitator writes the vision or goal the team wants to acheive on flip chart paper.
3. Using 5″ × 8″ cards, the team works to identify areas of agreement.
4. Then the team identifies areas of disagreement.
5. Each person writes what changes will make agreement possible and posts these as well.
6. The team leader or facilitator helps the team work through a collaborative process to come to consensus.
7. Each team member will be able to say, "I support this decision although it may not be my first choice."

Time Required

Depends on the depth of the disagreement.

Tips for Best Use

- Sticky notes are a good alternative to cards.
- This tool for building consensus is good to use whenever there is substantial disagreement among team members.

Expected Results

The team will make decisions that all members can support, and in this way, they will avoid the problems that can arise when there is unresolved disagreement between team members. When a team makes decisions that everyone can support, they make faster progress toward the checkered flag. The team will become more skilled at building consensus as time passes and will be able to do it much more quickly or realize more quickly that a particular decision will not work.

A Real-Life Example of Successful Consensus

A project team in a major utility learned to reach consensus with great success. The company needed a way to attract young people to their transportation maintenance apprenticeship program. They decided to create and support a mentor program to work with youth attending local vocational schools. Conflicts and differences about how to accomplish this goal naturally surfaced, but the group managed them as they worked. By focusing on their vision and using 5″ × 8″ cards, they brainstormed ideas, identified tasks, and matched those tasks to the roles of staff and union employees. As a result, the team has shown early success in recruiting new mentors and mentees.

Caution Flag

Some people might suggest this process for reaching consensus, even when it isn't appropriate, because it works so well.

Two Real-Life Examples

For example, a school administrator was very pleased with early progress in implementing teacher involvement at his school. In fact, early outcomes of problem solving and decision making had been successful. One ad hoc group working on a community relations marketing plan was stuck, and tempers had begun to flare. The school administrator called in the outside facilitator to "bring the group to closure." The facilitator suggested that since this issue revolved around compensation for both hourly and salaried staff, perhaps the administrator should make the decision himself. At the principal's insistence, the facilitator met with the group and "facilitated" a consensus decision, which recommended a very expensive outcome. The ad hoc group sent the decision to the administrator, who rejected it. This outcome was not a surprise.

The lesson: Compensation issues are management decisions. The team should limit its decision-making responsibility to those issues within its own domain to resolve, and leave other decisions to the responsibility of the designated leader.

Ned Jarrett tells the story of the Dale Jarrett stock car team, which was having difficulty with slow pitstops and uncompleted tasks. Robert Yates, the team owner, decided to hire an athletic trainer to pump up the pit crew. One person balked. He believed he already worked hard enough in the garage and on race day, and he didn't want to work out. Because just one team member resisted, no consensus existed, and the team showed no improvement in their performance.

This particular case of failure to reach consensus has a happy ending. Robert Yates hired Jeff Gordon's former Pit Crew (special team) to work only in the pits, and left this garage team to focus on their job. This splitting of responsibility has proven to be a highly successful outcome. The one crew person who resisted motivated the team to explore other, more creative, solutions than the one they originally had in mind.

Clearing Obstacles to Success

Often within an organization, there are systems, people and politics in existence that make the work of the team more difficult than it has to be. When a team is working hard yet seems stuck—and team members are spinning their wheels— a Force Field Analysis can help them determine their points of leverage. Originally developed by Kurt Lewin in 1951, the Force Field Analysis identifies the forces that keep a given situation in place, as well as those that are pushing for change.

What's Driving This Car?
(Force Field Analysis)

Materials

- Flip chart paper
- Markers

Procedure

1. The team leader or facilitator writes the issue or decision across the top of a piece of flip chart paper and labels it "Present State."
2. Through discussion, the team determines the "Desired State" or vision and writes this under the first statement.
3. The team leader or facilitator then draws a vertical line down the middle of the flip chart paper, and labels each of the two columns. One column is "Driving Forces" and the other "Restraining Forces."
4. The team brainstorms ideas to identify the various forces, both forces "for" and forces "against." The team leader or facilitator writes these ideas in the appropriate column.
5. The team then weights each item by drawing arrows of various lengths and weights to represent the strength of the various forces. Weighting is important because it's easy to generate a list of negative ideas that seems longer and more powerful than the forces for the change.
6. The force or forces with the longest and thickest arrows have the most power and possibly offer the greatest leverage.

7. Once the patterns have become clear, the team can work together to determine what next steps it will take to reduce negative forces and/or work more effectively with positive ones.

8. Questions the team may want to discuss include:
   a. Who in our system has access to the force that we're trying to change?
   b. Which force, if we change it, will cause repercussions in the organization?
   c. What are these possible repercussions?
   d. What are our available resources?
   e. Where do we have the most leverage?

Time Required

1–2 hours

Tips for Best Use

- The team needs plenty of time for the brainstorming activity. It's important that they think of as many forces as possible to create the most options for action.

- Many teams will choose to both lessen some negative forces and add to the positive forces—an eclectic approach.

- Though Lewin demonstrated that lessening negative forces often had more impact than strengthening positive ones, no set rule exists to determine how a team should proceed. Instead, successful teams look at their particular problem and determine together where the points of greatest leverage are. Then they concentrate their energy and efforts at these points.

Expected Results

Using *What's Driving This Car?* helps teams take a step back from their work and take a look at the whole picture. They may see that they've been expending energy trying to change what they actually have little ability to change. They may be able to see solutions or find leverage that they were unable to see before. They will refocus their energy on a task that will produce more solid results or get the team unstuck.

Example of the Use of "What's Driving This Car?"

The following example comes from a department manager's work. She wanted to explore the feasibility of changing to a more self-directing work environment. She wanted to uncover any resistance and see what it would take for her team to support this change.

> **PRESENT STATE:** We operate with functional roles and responsibilities and hierarchical decision making.

> **DESIRED STATE:** We operate in a self-directing business environment. Roles and responsibilities are based on individual strengths and skills, and we make decisions jointly.

Example of *What's Driving This Car?*
(Force Field Analysis)

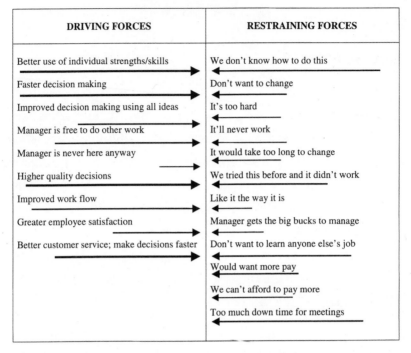

DRIVING FORCES	RESTRAINING FORCES
Better use of individual strengths/skills	We don't know how to do this
Faster decision making	Don't want to change
Improved decision making using all ideas	It's too hard
Manager is free to do other work	It'll never work
Manager is never here anyway	It would take too long to change
Higher quality decisions	We tried this before and it didn't work
Improved work flow	Like it the way it is
Greater employee satisfaction	Manager gets the big bucks to manage
Better customer service; make decisions faster	Don't want to learn anyone else's job
	Would want more pay
	We can't afford to pay more
	Too much down time for meetings

The four heaviest and longest arrows on the driving forces side suggest good reasons to make the change to the desired state.

Looking at the arrows, the manager can see some resistance to the change. This doesn't mean she shouldn't move in this direction, though. It *does* mean she needs to plan carefully and prepare thoroughly. The four heaviest and longest arrows on the driving forces side suggest good reasons to make the change: better and faster customer service; better and faster decisions overall; and better use of the team's strengths and skills.

To be successful, she needs to include her office department in planning self-directed team training, coordinating cross-training, tracking milestones and celebrating success. Involving everyone in the Fast Start Teamwork™ tasks and activities will support the driving forces and weaken the restraining forces at the same time.

Going back to the CARStyles™ assessment her team completed previously, the manager knows the *Utility Vehicle* will want some details: Who else has done this? What happened? How long did it take? The *Full Size Sedan* will want to know the bottom line outcome for other departments who've tried moving to self-direction and will ask, "How much of my time will this take away from other work?" The *Sporty Coupe* will immediately begin brainstorming resources and activities to get started faster. The *Minivan* will be slow to take action, but will volunteer to make meeting arrangements and call other people who've already tried self-directing methods.

Knowing What the Team Can Influence

A tool similar to *What's Driving This Car?* is useful in determining those elements within the team's control to change.

Control/No Control

A simple and quick way to identify forces that the team can change is to use flip chart paper divided lengthwise into two columns. The team leader or facilitator writes on top: "Control" and "No Control." The team brainstorms items for both sides. The Control issues are those the team can change or improve. The No Control issues are outside the team's domain of influence. The idea is to let those items go and focus the team's energy on what they can control.

Measuring Team Cohesion

When the team first came together, they took an inventory, *Take a Team Test Drive*, to assess their status as a team. This inventory gave them a base line from which to measure the team's progress. Repeating the assessment will measure their improvement.

Take a Team Test Drive, *Revisited*

Materials

Copies of *Take a Team Test Drive* (see page 209)

Procedure

1. Each team member completes the questionnaire individually.
2. The team leader or facilitator tallies the scores and computes the average and the range.

3. The team compares the average score and the range on this assessment to these same measures on the first version of the activity and together respond to the following questions:

—How has the team improved?

—In what ways does the team still need to improve?

—What issues does the team need to address?

—What are the next steps the team wants to take?

Time Required

5–10 minutes for the assessment

Up to an hour to debrief

Tips for Best Use

- Team members fill out the questionnaire without any help from anyone or conversation with anyone.

- The team can do another activity while the team leader or facilitator tallies up the scores and computes the team averages—or they can complete the questionnaire at one meeting and debrief at the next.

Expected Results

The team will most likely be pleased with the progress they've made. If this is the case, they can use the results as a basis for planning a celebration or taking on new challenges. If the team finds that it hasn't achieved the desired results, they need to acknowledge this and consider a time of reflection (see *It's Time for a Tune-up,* page 172).

Caution Flag

Again, some team members won't like the emphasis on numbers. The team needs to take care not to point fingers if the numbers don't show the improvement they'd hoped for. Assessments like *Take a Team Test Drive* are by their nature somewhat subjective. Also, as scores improve, the expectation of the group being surveyed goes up, therefore raising the bar. Team members need to understand the usefulness of the assessment—and the limits to its usefulness, as well.

A Real-Life Business Case

The union-management team mentioned previously used its own *Take a Team Test Drive* survey to assess and track results. They identified areas for improvement. They formed various teams to study each issue more deeply and make improvement recommendations. The group had committed to a follow-up survey within six months. The second survey produced lower scores on several items. Upon reflection, team members could identify several factors outside the control of the plant that had adversely affected the scores. Because of this, they did not become disheartened.

Refocusing the Team's Attention on the Vision

A racing team will rarely lose sight of their vision—they want to win the race and the championship. In business,

Teams sometimes ignore the signals that let them know they're no longer making progress toward their vision, such as a growing competition between team members.

however, sometimes a team may need to refocus their attention on the vision. This way, they won't get discouraged and quit. They also won't decide that the vision was too much of a stretch and accept a lesser vision in its place. A Gap Analysis such as *How Many Laps to Go?* works to refocus the team's attention on the vision and give them renewed energy for their work.

When a race driver is speeding around the track, experience and systems in the automobile tell the driver that an adjustment is needed: The car may need new tires, a tank of gas, or actual repairs. The key is that the driver recognizes the need and *will not continue racing* until the need is met. The driver knows that to do so will cause the team to lose the race or perhaps even hit the wall.

In the business world, because an urgent "must-do-now" issue or crisis erupts, teams sometimes ignore the signals that let them know they're no longer making progress toward their vision, such as growing competition between team members. These crises can even distract the team completely rather than stop it only temporarily. If a team fails to identify and take care of gaps between where they are and where they want to be, the team will ultimately fail to achieve its vision and will not add the intended value to the organization.

How Many Laps to Go? (Gap Analysis)

Materials

- Copy of the team's vision statement
- Flip chart
- 5" × 8" cards
- Markers
- Masking tape

Procedure

1. The team leader or facilitator posts the team's vision statement on the wall or writes it on a flip chart.
2. Team members individually use their cards to describe the team's current status in regard to the vision. What parts has the team achieved? What parts do not yet exist? Team members write one idea per card.
3. Working together, team members place the cards beneath the appropriate portion of the vision statement. They then use the ideas on the cards to identify the gap between current reality and the vision.
4. A team member creates a handout with the vision statement at the top and the list of gaps below and distributes a copy to team members.

Time Required

Approximately one hour

Tips for Best Use

- It's important to have the team's vision statement in front of the team throughout this exercise. The team leader or facilitator can call the team's attention to it if they seem to be straying off-track.

- Sticky notes are a good alternative for this activity.

- Team members may want to discuss why they haven't achieved their vision. Using *What's Driving this Car?* may be appropriate (see page 153).

Expected Results

Team members will identify the gaps between what they want to create and where they are now. They can use this information to adjust their strategy accordingly.

Caution Flag

Team members could lose hope if the gaps are wide. The team leader's task is to motivate them to look at their situation from a different perspective and to focus on what they *have* accomplished rather than only on what they haven't. Often, they can reframe the gap as an opportunity to take a different approach or learn new skills.

Two Tires or Four? (Adjusting the Strategy)

A common strategic decision the driver and the pit crew make during a race is whether to change two tires or four. All new tires give the car greater speed and stability on the road, but putting them on takes precious seconds. The conditions of a particular race will determine the best strategy.

Business teams may need to make quick strategic team adjustments as well. *FAST™ Problem Solving* works well for this purpose. The difference is that instead of solving a problem exterior to the team, now the team will take a FAST™ look at themselves. "Where you look is where you will go" applies internally as well as externally.

Materials

- A copy of the team's vision statement
- The results of *How Many Laps to Go?* on flip chart paper or handouts
- A copy of *FAST™ Problem Solving* for each team member

Procedure

The team documents the evidence of the Felt Need (slow progress toward the vision) and establishes measures to indicate success, such as increased attendance at meetings, or an obstacle to process removed.

The team analyzes the problem by gathering data. They can redraw process maps if they think their problem lies in the process they use. Or they can bring potentially painful interpersonal issues to the surface and begin to deal with them. A *What's Driving This Car?* session might be useful (see page 154). They need to ask "Why?" over and over again until they're sure that they've found the root cause or causes of the problem that has them stalled.

The team now brainstorms possible creative solutions to the problem. The group *does not* judge the solutions at this point. Rather, they encourage people to think creatively and make it safe for them to say whatever pops into their minds.

The team needs to look at the problem from multiple perspectives and call in resource people if necessary. Resource people may include front-line people.

By consensus, the team chooses what appears to be the best solution, tests it on paper, and implements it.

They test the results according to pre-established measures to see if they've solved the problem. If so, they celebrate. If not, they go back to Step 2 and try again.

Expected Results

The team will get back on track and find new energy to pursue the vision. The collective energy and collaborative spirit of the team will have its members ready to take go around the track again.

Caution Flag

The team leader or facilitator needs to encourage the team not to dwell on what's gone wrong and guide them to what they need to be doing. The time the team spends over-analyzing what went wrong is time spent not focusing on the work they need to do.

Celebrating Success

It's quite important to celebrate when a team reaches milestones and/or achieves its vision. The celebration marks the end of a particular project or part of one. It brings the group together and helps them cement relationships, and it's fun.

Teams may also want to reward themselves in other ways—by shared meals, or purchases of various kinds. One way to decide how to celebrate is to use the *Let the Driver Decide* technique.

Banners like this one help keep everyone in the "team frame of mind."
They remind team members why celebrating is in order.

Let the Driver Decide

Materials

- A figure of a race driver drawn in simple outline form on a piece of flip chart paper
- Markers

Procedure

1. The team identifies the goal of the celebration.
2. The team leader or facilitator posts the outline figure of a race driver on the wall.
3. Team members brainstorm ideas for celebrating. The team leader or facilitator writes down all ideas—one on each of the driver's arms, a few on the legs, one or two on the torso, one on the head.
4. Based on the goal, the team identifies criteria for success, or limitations, such as money.
5. By consensus, the team eliminates those ideas that don't fit the criteria and chooses one that does.

6. The team creates an action plan for the celebration and makes it happen.

Tips for Best Use

- Everyone who will be affected by the outcome needs to be involved. The team leader or facilitator might post the "driver" in the lunch area for others to add their ideas.
- Criteria for success might include "something all shifts can participate in."
- Team members will want to let go and have fun with this one.

Time Required

About 30 minutes

Expected Results

The team will select a way to celebrate for themselves, and consequently, they may enjoy the celebration more. They'll have a good time or receive an award, and, as a result, they'll be more motivated to work toward achieving their goals.

Caution Flag

The biggest difficulty is leaving out someone's preference for celebration. People with different personalities and styles of communication like to celebrate in different ways. Most of the time, those who disagree will understand and won't block the enjoyment of others.

Real-Life Celebration Examples

- Robert Yates and Dale Jarrett set aside a percentage of their winnings to award to the crew when they won the Winston Cup championship.

- Most race drivers celebrating in the winner's circle climb on the roof of their car and spray the beverage of the day all over the crowd of well-wishers and crew.

- Management cooked hamburgers for all three shifts at a plant that improved its quality rate.

- A team leader came through the team work area after the team had completed a successful project with peanuts, caramel corn, and tickets for the team to attend an afternoon baseball game together.

- A small office team went out to dinner together with their guests.

- A management team bought jackets for all team members to celebrate a successful emergency response.

- A team leader rented an ice cream cart and pushed it through the team area, offering a refreshing break to team members who had worked long and hard on a project.

- One company staged a team fair. Booths provided a place where teams could demonstrate and display their successes. Everyone in the plant took two to three hours to stroll through the exhibits and congratulate team members. This event was a day of learning for all employees as well as a day of fun.

laps to go!

8

Continuous Improvement– Racing Again . . . Better

"No successful person in racing, or in business, ever believes the job is done. There's always more you can do to make your team, your car, your business the best it can be."

—Gene Haskett, President, Michigan International Speedway

FIGURE 16: A Guide for Chapter 8—Continuous Improvement

Steps Along the Pathway to the Checkered Flag	Fast Start Teamwork™ Tools	Location in this Chapter
Evaluate the team's experience and identify what they've learned	Time for a Tune-up	Page 172
Share what they've learned with the organization	Spread-the-Word Checklist	Page 177
Make changes in the team as required	CARStyles™ Inventory *Revisited*	Page 67, Chapter 4
	Shifting Gears	Page 180
Start a new project at a higher level of performance	What Kind of Car Are You? (Go back to the Forming/ Orientation Stage)	Page 44, Chapter 4

Successful Teams Take Time to Reflect

A major measurable difference between successful teams and teams that are less successful is whether they have a regular debriefing after each project. Taking time to think together about what went right, what went wrong, and what changes the team wants to make can make all the difference in their next trip around the track.

One of the regrets George Winchester and Russ Yeager mentioned was that they failed to document the process they used the first time they worked together. They lost the opportunity to document continuous improvement, which, they believe, would have speeded the process the second time.

Time for a Tune-up*

Materials

- Flip chart
- Sticky notes in various colors, one color for each question
- Markers

---

* Based on a design by Dale Schreiner, DTE Energy Process Improvement Specialist. Used with permission.

Procedure

1. The team leader or facilitator writes the questions to think about on the flip chart. He or she writes one question per page and posts these around the room, allowing enough space for a group to work near the page. Team members may want to add a question or two to the list. The team can choose four or five questions that interest them most from the list below:

   - What was your understanding as to the purpose of this project?

   - What was a personal expectation you had when the project started?

   - What are the rough spots you encountered as you worked with this team?

   - What worked really well as you worked with this team?

   - What would you like to say to this team you haven't said yet?

   - What are the most important lessons you learned from working with this team?

   - What piece of advice would you give to the next team doing a similar project?

   - What would've made the work itself go better?

2. Each team member has several sticky notes in each color. For each question, each team member writes one or more responses, one response per note. The team member or the facilitator can then post the responses under the question.

3. The team numbers off to divide into as many groups as there are questions.

4. Each group gathers beside one of the questions to analyze the data and sort the answers into themes. Logical groupings will occur.

5. Each group reports back to the larger group what themes they found and what they learned from their analysis of the data.

6. Finally, the team leader or facilitator leads the group in discussing all the information and in generating a list of desired changes.

Time Required

Two to four hours—at least one to respond to questions, at least one to debrief. Depending on the nature of the project they've completed, team members may want more time.

Tips for Best Use

- It's important that team members choose the questions they want to discuss or at least have the opportunity to add to the list the team leader or facilitator has prepared.

- Team members need time for plenty of discussion.

Expected Results

Team members will think about the project they've completed and begin to understand it better. Consciously analyzing the project as a group will encourage them to improve their way of working together or change their approach. This will tend to lead to continuous improvement in the team's performance.

Caution Flag

Because it doesn't contribute tangibly to a work product, many teams find reflection an easy step to omit. Yet it may be one of the most important parts of teamwork that adds real value to the organization. Also, it's easy to generate a list of possible improvements the team wants to make, but not so easy to implement the improvements. The team needs to prioritize its list, and then select one or two improvements to make and concentrate on those. If the team tries to do it all, they may wind up making no significant changes at all.

A Real-Life Story of Reflection

An acquisitions and merger team worked together to prepare a bid to acquire another company. They worked long, hard hours and did careful analysis, yet their final bid fell far short of the winning bid. The team leader wanted to know how the team felt and what they'd like to do differently next time. They

WISDOM FROM ANOTHER RACING SPORT

Adventure racers are serious about feedback. One team member describes the process this way: "We let go of a decision once it's been made—no matter how it turns out. You have to treat mistakes as the next challenge, rather than as a self-inflicted problem. That doesn't mean that there isn't plenty of post race feedback. We come back after each race and analyze every decision in a very honest and pretty raw fashion. We talk about why people acted the way they did, why we made particular decisions, and how we ended up in particular circumstances." Each session like this helps the team learn and make better decisions the next time around.

called in an internal consultant to conduct an *It's Time for a Tune Up* workshop.

The team was able to determine that their competitors were using a different system for valuing the company they were trying to acquire. While they didn't decide to change their style, they *did* come to understand that using it put them at a disadvantage in the merger and acquisitions market.

Sharing Learnings With the Organization

Many companies have formal ways to share information, such as newsletters or sites on the company's intranet. The checklist below offers the team some suggestions for ways to share what they've learned with others. Team members may have other ideas to add to the list.

Spread-the-Word Checklist

_____ Some Ford Motor Company teams maintain a "Team Room" website accessible to team members only. With this site, team members can keep others at other locations updated on progress reports. Does your team have access to such a website?

_____ If not, can the team create a similar site?

_____ Is there a newsletter that accepts "Lessons Learned" pieces a team member can write?

_____ Is there a site on the company's intranet that accepts "Lessons Learned" pieces?

_____ Has the team asked new team members for any suggestions they might have based on their previous experience?

_____ If you're a new team member, have you offered to share with the team what you learned on your last project?

_____ Can the team make a formal presentation about their work to a leadership group?

_____ Can the team send e-mail updates to other teams involved in similar projects or to the team champion?

_____ Can a team member coach or mentor someone else in the organization?

_____ Is there a forum within the organization that enables representatives from various teams to meet and talk about their progress and successes?

_____ Can a team member attend round-tables and town hall meetings and present information there?

_____ Can a team member get on the agenda for a staff meeting?

_____ Can team members post charts and graphs that show their progress in a highly visible place?

Making Changes in the Team as Required

Changes of all kinds are a normal part of life. As Ben Blake, senior editor for *Racer* magazine, says, "Life, and racing, don't follow straight lines."

While people cannot necessarily anticipate all changes nor avoid the uncertainty that accompanies them, they *can* have planned ways to deal with change, such as a transition process to follow when team membership or team leadership changes. Such a process will help ease the pain and maintain the team's integrity.

RACING WISDOM

"The big problem is that the picture is always changing. What worked for Dale Earnhardt in '78 won't work today. What worked for Jeff Gordon in '90 likely wouldn't work today either."

—Ernie Irvan, NASCAR driver and Daytona 500 winner

Shifting Gears When the Makeup of the Team Changes

A Change in Team Leadership

When team leadership changes, several things can happen:

- The team may have to face feelings of ambiguity and confusion.
- Team members may alter their behavior beyond what is acceptable to the group.
- The team may revert to an earlier stage of development.
- Role structure may change.
- Team members may resist the change and demonstrate their resistance in various ways.

As a result, the team may become ineffective in their ability to solve problems, and their productivity may diminish. Conflict may increase.

Two Real-Life Leadership Change Stories

Here, George Winchester shares his view on change in team leadership. George begins, "When a new plant manager or leader comes in, already there's an expectation that there's a reason that person was brought in. So there's some energy for change. I say to people, 'I'll share with you my philosophy and how I think we've got to go, and at the same time, you tell me why you think it's important what you're doing.' Russ [Yeager] and I use a sit-down discussion format to listen to people's concerns and ideas."

George continues, "We quickly understand things and get quick agreement that the status quo is not going to work. We have these agreed-to things in place, we have to focus on the right issues, and we have to change quickly. I think you have to move as quickly as you can, but not so fast you don't do it [the change process] justice."

George summarizes, "As the new leader, you start out very quickly; it's your obligation. Stephen Covey says, 'Seek first to understand and then to be understood.' Spend time on real-time data collection, do the up-front visioning, team-building from the top leadership team, and put in place the building of strong leaders throughout."

In contrast, a plastic components automotive supplier is privately owned and employs about 300 people. They had an effective team-oriented employee participation process. There was a joint management and hourly steering committee, and everyone had been trained in teamwork and problem solving. Results included significant improvement in both customer and supplier relations, and establishment of a visual management system.

Suddenly, the out-of-state individual owner hired a new sales person to be president. He demoted the existing president to vice president, and the vice president to plant manager. The new plant manager was moved from his carpeted office onto the shop floor.

Just as suddenly, rumors began to fly that the plant was being sold. All interest in steering committee meetings, quality, and process improvement activities vanished. The word was,

"Since they're selling the plant, and we'll all lose our jobs, what's the point?"

A structured "Team Leader Transition Process" with the out-of-state owner in attendance might have prevented the downturn in productivity and process improvement and the eventual exodus of workers to other nearby plants.

Team Leader Transition Process

Logistics

- A room large enough for a meeting with the new leader, the old leader and the team
- Refreshments if appropriate, as food often makes occasions like this easier

Procedure

1. The outgoing team leader can begin the meeting by describing the Transition Process, but it is often better if an outside facilitator conducts the meeting.
2. The outgoing team leader can introduce the incoming team leader to the team. This is the symbolic passing of the torch.
3. Consider using a Check In at this point to set the tone for the rest of the meeting and make team members feel as if they have a voice.
4. Either the new team leader or the outside facilitator leads the team in a dialogue about the change in leadership, about issues concerning the future focus for the organiza-

tion or department, and about the goals and priorities that will maintain or improve the team's effectiveness.

5. The new team leader and team members exchange expectations.

6. The new team leader closes with remarks that may include comments about leadership style, preferences and philosophy, and then the new team does a Check Out to close the meeting.

A Change in
Team Membership

When there is a change in team membership, a team will typically go back to an earlier stage of team development. According to William Bridges in *Managing Transitions*, the team will experience repercussions because of the change, and they may require some coaching to handle their feelings well. Again, an established transition process can help.

Team Member
Transition Process

When a team gains a new member, they may have lost an old one. Again, according to Bridges, the team will experience repercussions such as grief.

It is acceptable to identify "missing" strengths as a result of the loss of a member. However, it is very likely the team may have replaced these strengths with cross-training.

To facilitate the entry of the new team member or members, involving the new member immediately is key. The team can review the processes they used previously and include the new team member in them. Examples include the following:

- CARStyles™ Inventory—After the team member has been around for a couple of weeks, the team uses the inventory to determine the new person's style— and they add the new person to the profile. They will also review with him or her the meaning of the four styles and explain why teams work better if they have representation from all four quadrants of the matrix.

- Identity Poster—The team works together, including the new member, to make changes that include the new person.

- The Team Strength Profile—The team has a brief session in which they add the new person's strengths and preferences to the lists they generated before.

- FAST™ Problem-Solving Process—The team shows the new person how the process works and how to use it. They may want to describe its use and results they achieved.

- Mission, Vision and Goals—The team will want the new person to know about its mission, its vision and its goals, both short-term and long-term. How will the new person fit in? What will his or her role and responsibilities be?

A Real-Life Story of Change

When Ray Evernham left the Hendrick Motorsports Jeff Gordon #24 Team to head up the Dodge effort to return to NASCAR racing, Brian Whitesell replaced him. Apparently contradicting the "orming" model, the new team won the two races that followed the change. However, according to Ned Jarrett and others, the team was merely running the "Evernham program set-up." Dean Daugharthy of *Track Time* says, "Certainly the team wanted to do well for Brian, and they probably put extra effort into it."

Under Whitesell's guidance, the team finished 12th, 11th, 10th, and 10th for the season's final races. Late in the year, the team owner hired a new crew chief, Robbie Loomis. Whitesell became team manager and handles overall management duties. The following season, Jeff Gordon acknowledged that his new team needed time to adjust. "There have been changes," he said, "and we had to come together again."

Dealing with Changes Out of the Team's Control

It is useful for the team to identify those changes out of the their control, but not to be discouraged by them. The team can reframe many of these changes as an opportunity or force for improvement. Otherwise, they can put their time and energy where they can make a difference. This is a good time to consider using *What's Driving This Car?* (see page 153) or a *Control/No Control* session. (See page 157).

Starting a New Project at a Higher Level of Performance

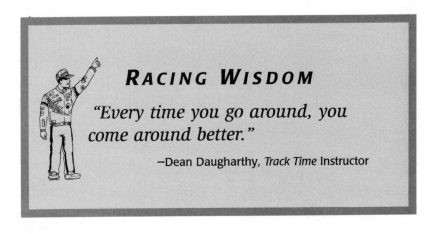

RACING WISDOM

"Every time you go around, you come around better."

–Dean Daugharthy, *Track Time* Instructor

As stated earlier, the "task" stages and the "interpersonal" stages of team development have a direct relationship. The matrix in the figure below shows the relationship.

A. A new team starting work on a completely new project is at the beginning stages of understanding team dynamics. They'll need to master their interpersonal relationships as well as achieve their goals. They can expect to go through all the stages of team development. They have much to learn and many opportunities ahead.

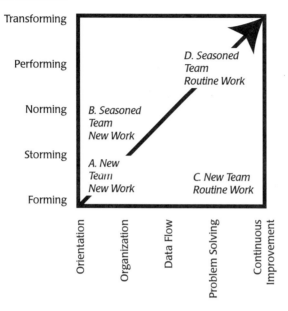

**Interpersonal
Social Relations**

Transforming

Performing — *D. Seasoned
Team
Routine Work*

Norming — *B. Seasoned
Team
New Work*

Storming — *A. New
Team
New Work* — *C. New Team
Routine Work*

Forming

Orientation Organization Data Flow Problem Solving Continuous Improvement

Task/Technical Functions

Teams can be at various stages of development and effectiveness.

B. A seasoned team that tackles a new work project does so at a higher level, because they've already worked through the interpersonal side of teamwork at least once. It's easier for them to focus on the steps of the task and achieve the vision they share, though new interpersonal challenges can always arise.

C. A new team working on a routine project with clearly defined tasks will need to pay attention to the interpersonal side of teamwork. Because the work is routine, unresolved interpersonal issues can take the team by surprise.

D. A seasoned team working on a routine project that they're familiar with will be able to carry the project to the continuous improvement stage. It's best not to wait until competition threatens to seek continuous improvement. Instead, successful teams use all their well-honed team skills to stay out in front as they head for the checkered flag and their trip to the winner's circle.

laps to go!

Standing in
the Winner's Circle

Teamwork for Life

"Two is better than one."

> —Rusty Wallace, speaking of his teammate, Jeremy Mayfield,
> for the Penske/Kranefuss two-car team

The steps in the preceding eight chapters guide a business team to do the following things:

- Get to know each other and appreciate each other's different communication and work styles

- Agree to their mission

- Create a shared vision

- Establish *Rules for the Road*

- Establish milestones by which to measure their progress

- Clearly define roles and responsibilities

- *Manage* rather than resolve conflict

- Make decisions by consensus

- Solve problems quickly and efficiently

- Get back on track if they've somehow gotten off

- Reflect on what they've learned in order to achieve continuous improvement and share their learnings in order to build their organization
- Appreciate the value of teamwork

A team like this one has used Fast Start Teamwork™ or other similar tools and has most likely taken the checkered flag.

In the introduction, we noted that team building does not apply only in the work place, but in our homes and communities as well. In fact, people can accomplish very few things in life all alone. Most of the time, we need help to achieve our goals. Acknowledging the importance of teamwork and building personal teams will help us succeed, both in business and in our personal lives. What follows are some examples of successful teams that have taken the checkered flag in non-business settings.

Teamwork Can Make Family Celebrations Flow More Smoothly

Family celebrations often carry with them a significant amount of work. Cooking Thanksgiving dinner, for example, can be quite a chore for one. One family has solved this problem with teamwork. All members of the family share a common vision—in their minds, they can see the turkey, dressing and vegetables on the table set for the holidays. Each one of them has a specific job to do. Mom cooks the turkey, makes rolls and prepares desserts the night before. Dad carves the turkey in the morning. One daughter sets the table. Another prepares the asparagus casserole. A third makes a relish tray and cooks her special mashed potatoes. Mom coordinates all this activity and adds the finishing touches. The family sits down to a wonderful meal around 2:00 p.m.—and no one is exhausted—all because of teamwork.

The chief characteristic of this family team is their shared vision. Each team member has a clearly defined role and responsibility—and they all celebrate when the job is done.

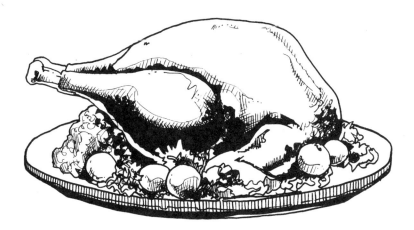

The shared vision this turkey represents is easy for family team members to imagine—and enjoy.

Teamwork Can Be an Answer to Community Problems

By forming teams in the community, we can solve problems. For example, working with a team, you can develop a hot air balloon festival that draws 10,000 people to your area or an art fair that draws half a million; conduct a capital fund campaign to create an educational component for young people to study classical music with the local symphony; or raise a million dollars to save a beloved scout camp from being sold for development.

In each of these cases, the teams have a compelling reason to devote their time and energy to teamwork. Like the family team, they share a clear vision and set goals to help them attain it.

Teamwork Can Work Deals with Those Who May Be Competitors

Race drivers sometimes team up to pass another competitor. The drivers know two cars can go faster together than they can go separately. So they draft, lining up one behind the other to pass a third car. In the business setting, we call it synergy.

For Ford Motor Company, several organizational development consultants worked together to deliver the RAPID improvement process to their mutual client. Working together, and with internal employees, they were able to reduce non-value-added work and improve cycle time that resulted in savings of over $400 million for Ford. These same consultants normally are friendly competitors, but for two years they worked together to help their mutual client achieve synergy and take the checkered flag.

Teamwork Can
Make School More Fun
and More Educational for Kids

A teacher wanted to teach his class about airplanes. He decided to build a mock cockpit in an unused doorway to the classroom. He got the children excited about the project. Each of them brought in materials and had certain parts of the project to complete. When they were done, they had a "cockpit" they could touch and manipulate, as well as an excellent experience of teamwork that one of those children remembers today, although this lesson occurred more than 15 years ago.

This teacher was an excellent team leader. He motivated his team members with a vision and found ways to put their individual skills and talents to use.

Teamwork Can
Make a Difference
in Other People's Lives

The Rotary Clubs in Jackson, Michigan, build access ramps for disabled children and adults. Rotary is an international service club based on membership by vocation classification, so the club has diversity by vocation. Educators, deans of local colleges, engineers, lawyers, cosmetic distributors, and car salesmen work side by side on projects because they share the Rotarian goal of "service above self." This team has achieved success 72 times since the project began. Perhaps their greatest success was when they built a ramp for a little girl who is disabled. Her only way out of the house was when someone first carried her wheelchair outside and then carried her out. It was clear that the teamwork of others had made a difference in her life when the tired Rotarians watched her wheel herself up and down the ramp, grinning from ear to ear with her new freedom.

The teamwork of others who built her ramp made a
dramatic difference in this young girl's life.

Teamwork Can Save Money

A city needed a new fire engine. The firefighters union knew that by buying two similarly equipped fire engines, a very large discount could be had. The union also knew a fire department in another city that needed a new engine. These two cities teamed up to place an order for two fire engines and split the discount.

Groups of people in cities across the nation team up to buy groceries in bulk at wholesale prices and save considerable amounts of money with teamwork. Mothers of young children team up in communities to form babysitting co-ops. And members of a subdivision come together on a Saturday morning to beautify the entrance to the residential area with flowers. Teamwork benefits all these people and their communities as well.

In cases like these, each participant receives greater value than he or she gives. Teamwork often has this effect.

Teamwork Is a Common Life Strategy

An especially simple and effective way we can practice teamwork is to accept the help of others when we need it. If we recognize ourselves and those who've helped us be successful as our personal teams, then we are more likely to take the checkered flag in our personal lives. We can build our personal teams by taking the time to say, "thank you." For example, a good way to say "thank you" to former teachers and professors is to write them a letter or offer to present a work-related experience to their classes. It takes very little time to say "thank you" to suppliers who go the extra mile for our businesses or to employees who do an outstanding job. And in just seconds a day, we can acknowledge the family members and friends—our teammates—who encourage us and help us along the way.

Publication Opportunity

- Do you have a great personal story about teamwork?
- Would you like to see your personal story in print?
- Would you like to share your story with others?
- We want to hear from you!

Our next book, *Checkered Flag Teams in Our Communities,* will tell how to make teamwork a way of life. We will share personal stories and examples of teamwork in various communities: family, neighborhood, and business, both local and global.

Please send us your true stories related to teamwork in any of these communities.

Please submit your typed story and a copy of this form with your signature:

Your name: _____

Address: _____

City: _____ State: _____ Zip: _____

Work Telephone: _____ or Home: _____

Email: _____

I understand that this submission becomes the property of the authors. I understand there is no guarantee my story will be printed.

(signature required) _____

Send to:

GOLD AND SILVER PRESS

4313 Joy Road West

Ann Arbor, MI 48105

Fax: (734) 426-3938

Email: jeroe@mail.com

Appendix A:
Reproducible Worksheets

The worksheets included here are for those tools in the book that require a worksheet to complete. Readers may reproduce them.

CARStyles™ Inventory

CARStyles ™ Self-Assessment

INSTRUCTIONS: Think of someone who knows how you behave at work. For list one, reading down, decide which word in each pair best describes your behavior **as they would describe it**. You may be some of both words, but what would the person you are thinking of say is the stronger behavior of the two? Circle or highlight the more appropriate word of each pair. Repeat the process for List Two.

LIST ONE			LIST TWO		
Fast paced	Or	Questioning	Steady	Or	Optimistic
Impatient	Or	Good listener	Practical	Or	Emotional
Candid	Or	Generous	Directive	Or	Inclusive
Challenger	Or	Unassuming	Reflective	Or	Considerate
Opinion-ated	Or	Compromis-ing	Reserved	Or	Impulsive
Demanding	Or	Watchful	Predictable	Or	Outgoing
Big-picture	Or	Deliberate pace	Pessimistic	Or	Supportive
Outspoken	Or	Precise	Rigid	Or	Talkative
Controlling	Or	Agreeable	Focused	Or	Relaxed
Evaluative	Or	Quiet	Rational	Or	Enthusiastic
Intense	Or	Detailed-oriented	Systematic	Or	Cheerful
Pushy	Or	Introverted	Blunt	Or	Cooperative
Dynamic	Or	Diligent	Cautious	Or	Flexible
Forceful	Or	Patient	Meticulous	Or	Stimulating
Action-oriented	Or	Non-judgmental	Depend-able	Or	Argumen-tative
TOTAL __		TOTAL __	TOTAL __		TOTAL __
*S		*A	*C		*R

Now total the selected words in each column. Select between *S or *A the number that is larger. Select between *C or *R the number that is larger. Combine the two higher scored letters to identify your prominent behavior style of communication. Plot your preferred style in the appropriate quadrant on the team profile.

CARStyles™ Matrix

*Control-oriented

<table>
<tr>
<td colspan="2">

CA

UTILITY VEHICLE
Melancholic

Detail-oriented

Proficient and Practical

Systematic and Dependable

</td>
<td colspan="2">

CS

FULL SIZE SEDAN
Choleric

Goal-oriented

Candid and Dynamic

Refined and Commanding

</td>
</tr>
<tr>
<td colspan="2">

RA

VAN
Phlegmatic

People and Team-oriented

Steady and Inclusive

Considerate and Supportive

</td>
<td colspan="2">

RS

SPORTY COUPE
Sanguine

Idea-oriented

Stylish and Spirited

Enthusiastic and
Imaginative

</td>
</tr>
</table>

*A
s
k
a
s
s
e
r
t
i
v
e

*S
t
a
t
e
a
s
s
e
r
t
i
v
e

*Relationship-oriented

Descriptions of the CARStyles ™ Quadrants

Utility Vehicle

Control-oriented and **A**sk-assertive people:

- Are conscientious and precise
- Are analytical and task-oriented
- Deal with facts, details, methods; want to know "how"
- Use standard operating procedures
- Prefer to avoid change
- Are conservative, low-key, and organized
- Are friendly, but aloof and guarded
- Tend not to show emotion; keep their distance
- Do not like superficial presentations
- Value accuracy and activity
- Are persuaded by facts, charts, graphs
- Learn best by practicing and working alone
- Make decisions slowly; prefer to share the risk
- Work at a cautious, deliberate pace
- Can be too cautious and impatient with others
- Under stress, may tend to withdraw, stall or over-analyze
- May need help to make decisions and move forward
- Send precise and punctuated e-mail messages
- Are dependable in providing facts and data to the team
- Want the team to achieve solutions without their involvement

Full Size Sedan

Control-oriented and State-assertive people:

- Are directing drivers and goal-oriented
- Move and speak quickly
- Are bottom line thinkers; want to know "what" and "when"
- Learn best by implementing actions and testing results
- Push for results; may become inflexible, rigid
- Like to take control of change and assume risk
- Under stress, may become pushy and rude
- Are independent and competitive
- Are persuaded with results, not testimonials
- Can be friendly, but formal and restrained
- Are professional; keep their distance
- Value results and forward progress
- Prefer action, efficiency, and quick decisions
- May avoid personal involvement with people
- Send concise and to-the-point e-mail messages
- Will challenge ideas and facts
- Will outwardly disagree with others
- Will challenge the team to do better
- Able to keep the goal in focus for others
- Tend to tell team members what to do

Sporty Coupe

Relationship-oriented and **S**tate-assertive people:

- Are expressive and idea-oriented
- Are able to influence and inspire others
- Are fast-paced, enthusiastic, and spontaneous
- Tend to show their emotions
- Tend to gesture and speak quickly
- Like to initiate relationships and partnerships
- Are quick to state their opinions
- Are quick to embrace change; see the big picture benefit
- Learn best by picturing the outcome
- Prefer options; want to know "who"
- Can be competitive and impatient
- Are talkative; sometimes a little loud
- Under stress, may overuse humor or attack the ideas of others
- Easily stray off-track
- Tend to value a show of sincere interest
- Like applause and personal recognition
- May want help from others, when needed
- May send e-mail message filled with color and fancy fonts
- Like to collaborate to achieve team goals
- Motivate the team by cheerleading

Minivan

Relationship-oriented and **A**sk-assertive poeple:

- Are steady, people- and team-oriented
- Are friendly, accepting, cooperative, open
- Tend to show their feelings, may hug others
- Like to ask questions; want to know "why"
- Are good listeners and use supportive words
- Like to be liked and enjoy sharing
- Tend to limit constructive feedback
- Learn best by interacting with a group
- Are persuaded with suggestions
- Under stress, may become quiet, give in or be super-agreeable
- Need to feel safe and like to reduce risk of failure
- Prefer structure over dynamic change
- Prefer agreeable, slow pace and soft voice
- Are slow to take action to change; may use short-term solutions
- Value relationships with others; enjoy small talk
- Need time to feel trust in another
- May hang back at first waiting for others; patient
- Send very friendly and chatty e-mail messages, in which the punctuation and capitalization may be spotty
- Ensure communication within the team
- Are motivated to help others on the team

Take a Team Test Drive

INSTRUCTIONS: For each component below, circle the number you believe represents where your team is now.

Vision and Goals

Lack of commonly						Members understand and			
understood vision and goals						agree on vision and goals			
1	2	3	4	5	6	7	8	9	10

Roles and Responsibilities

Often overlap and							Clearly defined;		
are unclear							clear boundaries		
1	2	3	4	5	6	7	8	9	10

Leadership

One or two people							Team members		
dominate							share leadership		
1	2	3	4	5	6	7	8	9	10

Team Member Contribution

Members' contributions are						Members' contributions are			
not recognized or used						fully recognized and used			
1	2	3	4	5	6	7	8	9	10

Interpersonal Communication

| Closed and guarded | | | | | | | Open and participative | | |
| 1 | 2 | 3 | 4 | 5 | 6 | 7 | 8 | 9 | 10 |

Conflict

Much disruptive conflict   Conflict is openly managed

1   2   3   4   5   6   7   8   9   10

Procedures

No procedures to guide   Effective procedures to
team functioning   guide team functioning

1   2   3   4   5   6   7   8   9   10

Problem Solving/Decision Making

No agreed-on approaches   Well-established and
to solve problems or   agreed-on approaches
make decisions

1   2   3   4   5   6   7   8   9   10

Creativity/Risk-taking

Rigid, does not explore   Taking a risk to try
new ideas or take risks   new ideas is supported

1   2   3   4   5   6   7   8   9   10

Self-evaluation

Group does not   Team often evaluates itself
evaluate itself   and makes improvements

1   2   3   4   5   6   7   8   9   10

Team Leader or Facilitator Instructions for *Take a Team Test Drive*:

1. Tally the scores from the worksheets and calculate the mean average. Also take note of the range from high to low.

low									high
1	2	3	4	5	6	7	8	9	10

2. If the average is 5.5, but one person scores consistently low, i.e., 2–3, while others are 5–7, there are other issues involved. This is an opportunity for open discussion about this situation without identifying individual scores.

3. These components of successful teams are suggestions only. You and your team may add or substitute questions.

4. After sharing scores with the team, facilitate a discussion of what the findings mean for the team. Identify one or two components to work on and improve.

High Octane Teams/
The Loyal Fan

INSTRUCTIONS: Working individually, respond to the following items. When completed, share this insight with your teammates.

1. My greatest contributions to this group will include:
   a. A technical skill or skills I offer:

   b: An interpersonal skill or skills I offer:

2. My hidden or unused talents include:

3. My preferences for work assignments include:

4. Some work assignments I really don't enjoy much include:

The Auto Parts Store Challenge

A man dressed in blue jeans and a plaid shirt went into an auto parts store to buy floor mats for his pick-up truck. The floor mats cost $13. He handed the store clerk a twenty-dollar bill; the man seemed in a hurry. It was just after opening, and the young clerk didn't have any change. The store clerk took the twenty-dollar bill and went next door to the office supply store, where he exchanged it for twenty one-dollar bills. The clerk then gave the customer his change. Later that morning the office supply storeowner came to the clerk and said, gruffly, "This is a counterfeit twenty-dollar bill." The clerk apologized profusely and took back the phony bill. He gave the office supply store owner two good ten-dollar bills.

Not counting the price of the floor mats, how much money did the auto parts store lose?

For solution, visit either of these websites: www.4DeltaSystems.com or www.goldandsilverpress.com

Go As Far As You Can

Tally Sheet

INSTRUCTIONS: For 10 successive pitstops, you and your partner will choose either tires or fuel. Each pitstop's payoff depends on the pattern of choices you have made.

PAYOFF SCHEDULE

4 Tires :	Lose 1 lap each
3 Tires :	Gain 1 lap each
1 Fuel :	Lose 3 laps
2 Tires :	Gain 2 laps each
2 Fuel :	Lose 2 laps each
1 Tire :	Gain 3 laps
3 Fuel :	Lose 1 lap each
4 Fuel :	Gain 1 lap each

Confer with your partner before each pitstop and make a *joint decision*. During pitstops 5, 8, and 10, you and your partner may first confer with the other partnerships at your table before making your joint decision.

Go As Far As You Can Tally Sheet

SCORE CARD

Round	Your Choice (circle)	Partnership's Pattern of Choices	Payoff	Balance
1	Tires Fuel	___Tires ___Fuel		
2	Tires Fuel	___Tires ___Fuel		
3	Tires Fuel	___Tires ___Fuel		
4	Tires Fuel	___Tires ___Fuel		
5	Tires Fuel	___Tires ___Fuel		
6	Tires Fuel	___Tires ___Fuel		
7	Tires Fuel	___Tires ___Fuel		
8	Tires Fuel	___Tires ___Fuel		
9	Tires Fuel	___Tires ___Fuel		
10	Tires Fuel	___Tires ___Fuel		

Bonus Round: Payoff x 3 (Round 5)

Bonus Round: Payoff x 5 (Round 7)

Bonus Round: Payoff x 10 (Round 10)

Team Leader or Facilitator Instructions for *Go As Far As You Can*:

Objectives

1. To simulate the differences between competition and collaboration in teams in a comapny with limited resources
2. To illustrate the impact of win-lose situations

Group Size

The group forms partnerships of 2–3 people each. Four partnerships at each table are ideal, but other variations are possible.

Time Required

Approximately one hour

Materials

- Copies of the *Go as Far as You Can* tally sheet for each partnership
- Pencils
- Flip chart paper
- Markers

Physical Setting

Ideally, sets of partners sit opposite each other at a table like the four directions on a compass, far enough away from each

other for strategy discussions to be confidential, and close
enough for the partenships to interact. A table tent for each
group lettered A, B, C, or D makes it easier to keep score.

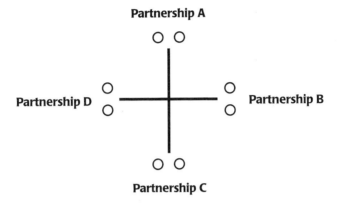

Process

1. Before beginning, the facilitator writes the payoff schedule
   on a flip chart.
2. He or she gives directions to divide into partnerships and
   gives each partnership a copy of the tally sheet.
3. The facilitator gives the following directions:

      "The title of this activity is 'Go as Far as You Can.' Keep
   that goal in mind throughout the experience. There are
   three key rules:

   a. Do not confer—either verbally or non-verbally—
      with members of the other partnerships at your
      table unless you are specifically told to do so.

   b. Each partnership must agree upon a single choice
      for each round.

c. Keep your choice a secret until the facilitator tells
      you to reveal it.

   There are 10 pitstops to this 'race.' During each pitstop,
you and your partner will have one minute to talk and mark
the choice you agree on for the pitstop. Remember the
rules. You may now take one minute to mark your choice
for pitstop one."

4. After about one minute, the facilitator should make sure
   that each partnership has completed the task before pro-
   ceeding. Then he or she says:

   "Share your partnership's decision with the other
   people at your table. Mark your score card on the tally sheet
   for round one according to the payoff schedule."

5. The facilitator asks if there are any questions before moving
   to round two.

6. The facilitator's response to all questions concerning the
   purpose of the activity is always, "The name of the game is
   Go as Far as You Can."

7. The facilitator continues the exercise by saying:

   "You have one minute to mark your decision for pitstop
   two." He or she waits a minute, then asks, "Has everyone
   made a selection?" If the response is yes, then he or she
   says, "Share and score your choices."

8. The facilitator continues the exercise by conducting pitstops
   three and four like pitstops one and two.

9. Round 5 is a bonus pitstop. The facilitator explains, "You will
   note that the tally sheet indicates that the score for this round
   will be multiplied by 3. Before you make your selection for
   this pitstop, you may discuss this exercise with the other
   members of your table group. After the group discussion, you

and your partner will have one minute to discuss your decision, as before. You may now have three minutes for group discussion." (The facilitator should stop the discussion after about three minutes.) The facilitator may notice that someone has figured out if they all pick "fuel" everyone gains one lap each. Even though the other partnerships may agree, they may or may not actually pick "fuel." Competition results.

10. The facilitator says:

    "Each partnership now has one minute to mark their decision for pitstop five. Remember the rules are now in effect—no talking across or under the table!"

    After about one minute, the facilitator checks to see that everyone has made a decision, and says:

11. "Share and score."

12. The facilitator conducts rounds six and seven like rounds one through four.

13. Pitstop eight is a bonus round, and the facilitator conducts it like pitstop five, with the score multiplied by 5.

14. He or she conducts pitstop nine like pitstops six and seven.

15. Pitstop ten is a bonus round. The facilitator conducts it like pitstop eight, with the score multiplied by 10.

16. The facilitator has each partnership compute its total score. People will want to brag about "winning."

17. The facilitator asks the groups to total the partnership scores at their table into one team score.

18. The facilitator debriefs by discussing the process and its implications. He or she might raise the following key points:

- Does the "You" in *Go as Far as You Can* mean you as a partnership or you as a group?

- What was the effect of competition and collaboration within our partnership and our organization?

- How does the group's net score compare to the possible net score of 100? (If each partnership agrees to "fuel" each time, the scores will be 25 + 25 + 25 + 25. Any other choices will produce a lower score.)

- How does this experience relate to other team situations?

- What social styles of communication were present for each round? Did people act as they would in a conflict or stressful situation?

- What other unusual situations occurred during the activity?

FINAL NOTE: There *can* be lingering hard feelings for cut-throat tactics people sometimes resort to in this exercise. The facilitator needs to allow ample time for debriefing. Remind people it's *only a game*, and that its purpose is to show how collaboration often gives better results than competition.

Appendix B:
Information About Racing

A Brief Explanation of NASCAR

The National Association of Stock Car Auto Racing (NASCAR®) is owned and managed by the France family. It was incorporated in 1948 and is the authority that sets rules and governs competition stock car racing and truck racing. NASCAR promotes many events including the Winston Cup Series, Busch Series, and Craftsman Truck Series. This entertainment experience is unrivaled in professional sports or in the entertainment world in terms of venues, participants, spectators and revenue.*

---

* A good resource for more information about the financial world of NASCAR is Robert Hagstrom's book, "The NASCAR Way," 1998.

NASCAR rules promote safety for the teams and the fans as well as ensure competitive racing and cost control for the teams. The rules govern all aspects of the sport before, during and after a race event. Each race week, the teams compete for the 43 race positions and 43 pits. They receive competition points for the pole position, laps led, and races won. Prize money is awarded for each race and at the year-end banquet.

The road to NASCAR involvement is as varied and as interesting as that of its founder, Bill France, Sr. Bill, Sr. and his wife, Annie B, made the perfect team to build an empire. Bill, Sr. was the visionary one, outgoing and outspoken. Annie B was the quiet, supportive half of this team. With the vision always in the forefront, NASCAR overcame opposition from a competing sanctioning body, automobile manufacturers, and the Environmental Protection Agency to achieve their vision. Bill, Jr. and James France now head NASCAR.

For drivers, the journey to NASCAR may start with a four-year-old boy driving a go-cart tethered to a stake in his backyard. Ken Schrader tells the story of how one day the rope broke, and he discovered he could "go anywhere he wanted to." Ken competes about 100 times a year wherever he can find a race. Many drivers start out on small dirt tracks in modified stock cars and gain enough skill to move on to high-speed ovals. In contrast, Winston Cup champion Dale Jarrett did not start racing until he was 20 years old.

Winston Cup series director Gary Nelson's journey began as a crew chief with a reputation for "inventiveness." He was a master at finding creative ways to boost engine power, or reduce drag. Some of these ways were outside NASCAR regulations. Many believe that his tendency to break NASCAR rules makes Gary the best at enforcing them.

For owners, the road may have been traveled as an assistant engine builder who eventually bought the team, as Robert Yates did. His racing business now includes two race teams and drivers, 85 employees, 40 cars and 70,000 square feet of garage space.

For fans, the road might start with the first trip to an oval, dirt track in Boone, Iowa. There, the fan hears the roar of the engines, sees the "door handle to door handle" racing, smells the engine oil in sharp contrast to the fresh, night air, and feels the excitement when the checkered flag waves over the race winner. He or she is most likely hooked forever.

Names Associated With Racing*

Brett Bodine	NASCAR driver, #11 Ford Taurus
Jeff Burton	NASCAR driver, #99 Exide Battery Ford Taurus
Dean Daugharthy	Instructor for *Track Time* Driving School. Builds and races cars with his father, Earl Daugharthy
Dale Earnhardt	NASCAR driver, seven-time Winston Cup champion, #3 GM Goodwrench Chevrolet; Car owner of #3 Busch Series car
Ray Evernham	Former crew chief for Hendrick Motorsports; owner of two-car Dodge Team

* Compiled by Dick Merchant

Henry Ford	Founder of Ford Motor Company. Built and drove a race car in 1901, and never raced again. Ford is the only automaker that can claim victory in the Indy 500, Daytona 500, 24 hours of LeMans and Daytona, 12 hours of Sebring, the Monte Carlo Rally, and the Baja 1000.
Bill (William Clifton) France, Jr.	Chairman and CEO of International Speedway Corporation. ISC is considered to be the undisputed leader in event entertainment.
Bill (William Henry Getty) France, Sr.	Founder of NASCAR and International Speedway Corporation. Deceased in 1992.
Jeff Gordon	NASCAR driver, three-time Winston Cup champion, #24 DuPont Chevrolet. Car owner of #23 Busch Series Pepsi Chevrolet
Gene Haskett	President, Michigan International Speedway
Richard Hilton	Owner of Hilton Racing and Brett Bodine's #11
Ernie Irvan	Retired Winston Cup driver
Dale Jarrett	NASCAR driver, Winston Cup champion, #28 Quality Care Ford Taurus
Ned Jarrett	Former NASCAR driver, two-time Winston Cup champion; broadcaster; businessman
Robbie Loomis	Crew Chief for Hendrick Motorsports, #24 DuPont Chevrolet

Jeremy Mayfield	NASCAR driver, #12 Mobil 1 Ford Taurus
Gary Nelson	Series Director for NASCAR Winston Cup, former crew chief, and Inventor of Record of race car roof flaps
Todd Parrott	Crew Chief for Robert Yates Racing, #28 Quality Care Ford Taurus
Benny Parsons	Winston Cup champion; first to drive a stock car over 200 miles per hour; broadcaster, awarded 1989 Cable ACE Award as the best sports analyst on cable television
Roger Penske	Former race driver; Vice Chairman, International Speedway Corporation; Chairman and CEO, Penske Corporation; founding director of CART (Championship Auto Race Teams); founder of Penske Racing South. His cars have won 100 races including ten Indy 500s, two Can-Am championships, three Trans-Am titles, numerous Winston Cup races, and one of only three Formula I Grand Prix races won by an American team
Richard Petty	NASCAR legend, three-time Winston Cup champion, winner of 200 races; car owner; broadcast commentator
Ken Schrader	NASCAR driver, #36 M&M's Pontiac
Rusty Wallace	NASCAR driver, Winston Cup champion, #2 Miller Lite Ford Taurus; winner of 100 races

Darrell Waltrip	NASCAR driver; three-time Winston Cup champion; broadcast commentator
Brian Whitesell	Crew Manager for Hendrick Motorsports, #24 DuPont Chevrolet
Robert Yates	Owner, two-car team, #88 Dale Jarrett and #28 Ricky Rudd

Racing Terms*

Banking	Degree of elevation of the racing surface; assists in keeping the cars safely on the track
Black Flag	Penalty flag; shown to bring a driver back to pit lane for consultation for infractions, such as, speeding on pit lane, or if smoke is coming from the car or sheet metal is hanging
Caution	Yellow flag; or a period in the race when the pace car leads the cars at a slower pace in order to allow cleanup of oil or debris after an accident
Crew Chief	Leader of the crew or race team
DNF	Did Not Finish; the car left the speedway without completing the race

---

* Compiled by Dick Merchant

Drafting	Two or more cars team up behind each other to take advantage of "towing effect" in order to go faster, to pass another car, or to save fuel
Groove	A race lane on the speedway; there is usually one groove that may be better for racing; the inside groove on an oval is the innermost line
Line	The point of the start/finish, or refers to groove or lane location on the speedway
Pit or pitstop	To bring the cars in for fuel, tires, adjustments
Pit Lane or Row	The area inside the track where the crews set up temporary garages during races so the driver can pit. There is often a speed limit to slow the cars down for safety of the crews.
Pole Position	The driver who drove the fastest lap in pre-race qualifying starts the race at the front, or in the pole position.
Scanners	One-way radios for fans and media to listen to the crew chief, driver, owner and spotter talk to each other
Spotter	A person with a *two-way* radio who sits in the grandstand and watches the speedway for the driver by looking ahead for accidents and advising alternate paths, and behind for cars who are

	gaining position; assists in passing by letting the driver know when cars are above or below the driver on the speedway.
Stock Car	Originally, this meant a regular car off the production line. Now, stock cars may have the exterior profile of a street car, but every other part is modified—the engine, horsepower, suspension, shocks and tires. Regardless of the manufacturer, all stock cars weigh a minimum of 3,400 pounds.
Straightaway	The straight portion and fastest part of a speedway.
Take the Checkered Flag	To cross the start/finish line with the checkered flag waving means the race is over; to be the first to take the checkered flag is to be the winner
White Flag	When two crossed white flags are shown, the race is half over; if one flag is flown near the end, this signifies one more lap to completion (checkered flag)
Winner's Circle	A place of celebration and the end of a race, may be a square-shaped area
Winston Cup	The Championship Cup trophy awarded to the winner at the end of the NASCAR season; there are also a banquet, money, and rings for the winning driver, spouse, and team members.

Appendix C: References

Articles

Benedetti, Marti. "Fast Cycle Time: Working Smarter." *Ford World,* July/August 1994.

Blake, Ben. "Grace Under Pressure," "Swing Shift," and "Making It." *1999 K-Mart 400 Official Race Program.*

Brown, John Seely and Gray, Estee Solomon. "The People Are the Company." *Fast Company,* November 1995.

Caminiti, Susan. "What Team Leaders Need to Know." *Fortune,* February 20, 1995.

Chengelis, Angelique S. "Two Is Better Than One." *The Detroit News,* June 15, 1998.

Johnson, Roy S., and Daniels, Cora. "Speed Sells." *Fortune,* April 12, 1999.

Kantor, Bob. "Letters to Fortune." *Fortune,* May 15, 1995.

Kaufman, Fred. "Leading Learning Communities." From a workshop conducted in 1996.

Kirsner, Scott. "Total Teamwork—SEI Investments." *Fast Company*, April 1998.

Labich, Kenneth. "Elite Teams Get the Job Done." *Fortune*, February 19, 1996.

Merchant, Renée. "Change, Choices, and Commitment." *The American Society of Training and Development Newsletter*, March 1997.

Roe, Jo Ellen, and Hermon, Mary Vielhaber. "Removing Barriers to Learning at Eastern Michigan University." *At Work*, July-August 1998.

Salter, Chuck. "Life In the Fast Lane." *Fast Company*, October 1998.

Verespej, Michael A. "America's Best Plants." *Industry Week*, October 20, 1997.

Wallace, Don, and McMurray, Scott. "How to Disagree (Without Being Disagreeable)." *Fast Comapny*, November 1995.

Books

Bridges, William. *Managing Transitions*. Addison-Wesley Publishing Co. 1991.

Center, Bill. *Ford Taurus in NASCAR*. Harper Collins Publishers. 1999.

Cox, Taylor, Jr. *Cultural Diversity in Organizations: Theory, Research and Practice*. Berrett-Kohler Publishers. 1993.

Dannemiller Tyson Associates. *Whole-Scale™ Change: Unleashing the Magic in Organizations*. Berrett Kohler Publishers. 2000.

Hagstrom, Robert G. *The NASCAR Way: the Business that Drives the Sport.* John Wiley and Sons, Inc. 1998.

Huler, Scott. *A Little Bit Sideways: One Week Inside a NASCAR Winston Cup Race Team.* MBI Publishing Co. 1999.

Huszczo, Gregory. *Tools for Team Excellence: Getting Your Team Into High Gear and Keeping It There.* Davies-Black Publishing. 1996.

Martin, Arlene, and Prensky, Janet. *Every Woman's Guide to Auto Racing.* Avery Publishing. 1999.

Martin, Bruce. *Stock Car Team Secrets.* MBI Publishing Co. 1999.

Senge, Peter. *The Fifth Discipline: The Art and Practice of the Learning Organization.* Currency Doubleday. 1990.

Stewart, Greg L., Manz, Charles C., and Sims, Harry P. *Team Work and Group Dynamics.* John Wiley and Sons. 1999.

Tuckman, B.W.; and Jensen, M.A.C. *Stages of Small Group Development Revisited.* Group and Organization Studies. 1977.

Varney, Glenn H. *Building Productive Teams.* Jossey-Bass Publishers. 1990.

Wallace, Rusty, and Zeller, Bob. *Rusty Wallace: The Decision to Win.* David Bull Publishing, Inc. 1999.

Movies and Audiotapes

Buckingham, Marcus and Coffman, Curt. *First Break All the Rules.* Abridged version. Simon and Schuster Sound Ideas. 1999.

Days of Thunder, 1990.

Personal Interviews

Androsian, Kevin. Detroit Edison. March 2000.

Daugharthy, Dean. *Track Time* Instructor. November 1999.

Jarrett, Ned. Jarrett Enterprises, Inc. November 1999.

Winchester, George. Jackson, MI. November 1999.

Yeager, Russ. Jackson, MI. November 1999.

Websites

www.4DeltaSystems.com

www.espn.com

www.fastcompany.com

www.fortune.com

www.goldandsilverpress.com

www.iscmotorsports.com

www.nascar.com

www.penskemotorsports.com

www.teamcenter.com

www.tracktime.com

INDEX

ABOUT THE AUTHORS

Renée Merchant

Renée Merchant is an independent business owner who seeks opportunities for teamwork. She founded Delta Systems in 1982 while earning a Bachelor of Business Administration and a Master of Science in Organization Development. She is highly regarded for her consulting skills and customized training programs that achieve bottom line results. Renée is a professional speaker and a contributing author to *Success Is a Team Effort*, James & Brookfield Publishers, 2000. She lives with her husband, Dick, at Lake Columbia near Michigan International Speedway. As avid race fans, they volunteer with the Pitstoppers team to cook lunch in the garage for drivers, crews, media, safety and track personnel during race events. Renée is a member of the Rotary Club of Jackson, Michigan and both are Rotary International Foundation Paul Harris Fellows.

Jo Ellen Roe

Jo Ellen Roe is the Communications Planner for the Culture Change and Communications team at Detroit Edison in Detroit, Michigan. In that capacity, she works with teams to develop, implement, and measure communications strategies. A former language teacher, she's been involved in numerous collaborative writing projects including four marketing booklets for University Housing at the University of Michigan and two annual reports for the Barriers to Learning initiative at Eastern Michigan University. She holds a Bachelor of Arts degree in English, a Master of Science in Education, and a Master of Science in Human Resources and Organization Development. She lives in Ann Arbor, Michigan with her husband, Chuck, and her youngest daughter, Holly. Since teaming with Renée, she has "tuned in" to the NASCAR world and is on her way to becoming a fan.

QUICK ORDER FORM

BILL TO:

Name: _____

Company: _____

Address: _____

City: _____ State: _____ Zip: _____

Telephone Number: _____

e-mail: _____

SHIP TO: *(complete only if different from "BILL TO" address)*

Name: _____

Company: _____

Address: _____

City: _____ State: _____ Zip: _____

Product Description	Quantity	Unit Price	Total Amount
Checkered Flag Teams: Driving Your Workplace to the Winner's Circle–6 x 9 Book, more than 30 activities		$19.95	
CARStyles ™ Starter Packet–1 Facilitator Guide plus 5 Participant Assessments & Guides		$50.00	
CARStyles ™ Facilitator Guide with training outline & overhead masters		$30.00	
CARStyles ™ Participant Assessment & Interpretation Guide–Sold in Packets of 5 guides		$30.00	
Face Poster Check-In Kit–Six laminated face posters		$15.00	
Success is a Team Effort–6 x 9 Book, 256 pages		$19.95	
Handling $4.00 first item, $3.00 each additional item			
Michigan Sales Tax: 6%			
TOTAL Enclosed			

METHOD OF PAYMENT:

❏ Check/Money Order   ❏ Visa   ❏ MasterCard   ❏ American Express

Card Number: _____ Exp. Date: _____

Signature: _____

❏ I would like information on consulting services and training programs related to Teamwork.

Thank you for your order!

Send payment to: **GOLD AND SILVER PRESS**
4313 Joy Road West, Ann Arbor, Michigan 48105, Fax: 734-426-3938

Order on our websites: www.goldandsilverpress.com or www.4DeltaSystems.com

QUICK ORDER FORM

BILL TO:

Name: _____

Company: _____

Address: _____

City: _____ State: _____ Zip: _____

Telephone Number: _____

e-mail: _____

SHIP TO: *(complete only if different from "BILL TO" address)*

Name: _____

Company: _____

Address: _____

City: _____ State: _____ Zip: _____

Product Description	Quantity	Unit Price	Total Amount
Checkered Flag Teams: Driving Your Workplace to the Winner's Circle—6 x 9 Book, more than 30 activities		$19.95	
CARStyles ™ Starter Packet—1 Facilitator Guide plus 5 Participant Assessments & Guides		$50.00	
CARStyles ™ Facilitator Guide with training outline & overhead masters		$30.00	
CARStyles ™ Participant Assessment & Interpretation Guide—Sold in Packets of 5 guides		$30.00	
Face Poster Check-In Kit—Six laminated face posters		$15.00	
Success is a Team Effort—6 x 9 Book, 256 pages		$19.95	
Handling $4.00 first item, $3.00 each additional item			
Michigan Sales Tax: 6%			
TOTAL Enclosed			

METHOD OF PAYMENT:

❑ Check/Money Order ❑ Visa ❑ MasterCard ❑ American Express

Card Number: _____ Exp. Date: _____

Signature: _____

❑ I would like information on consulting services and training programs related to Teamwork.   *Thank you for your order!*

Send payment to: **GOLD AND SILVER PRESS**
4313 Joy Road West, Ann Arbor, Michigan 48105, Fax: 734-426-3938

Order on our websites: www.goldandsilverpress.com or www.4DeltaSystems.com